Revision notes

Higher
English
revision notes

Larry Flanagan

Text © 2005 Larry Flanagan
Design & layout © 2005 Leckie & Leckie
Cover image © *Science Photo Library*

03/131207

ISBN 978-1-84372-283-0

Published by
Leckie & Leckie
3rd Floor
4 Queen Street
Edinburgh
EH2 1JE
Tel: 0131 220 6831
Fax: 0131 225 9987
E: enquiries@leckieandleckie.co.uk
W: www.leckieandleckie.co.uk

Special thanks to
Caleb Rutherford (cover design), Tony Wayte (copy edit), Rebecca Harman (proofreading)

A CIP Catalogue record for this book is available from the British Library.

® Leckie & Leckie is a registered trademark

Leckie & Leckie Ltd is a division of Huveaux plc.

All websites referred to in this book were checked and were correct and working at the time of going to press.

Leckie & Leckie has made every effort to trace all copyright holders. If any have been inadvertently overlooked, we will be pleased to make the necessary arrangements. We would like to thank the following for their permission to reproduce their material:
- Getty Images (images on pp. 7, 8, 16, 22, 25, 28, 44, 48, 57, 58, 60, 83, 99, 100, 103, 105, 110);
- Famous Pictures and Features Agency (image on p. 11);
- Scottish Viewpoint (photograph on p. 13);
- *The Independent* (article on pp. 22–23);
- Sean Coughlan, (*Sole Legends* page 25-26);
- Gordon Wright Scottish Photo Library (images on pp. 61, 64, 66);
- National Library of Ireland (Keogh Collection) (image on p. 62);
- Bloodaxe Books ('Pride' from *Off Colour* by Jackie Kay on pp. 69–70);
- 'Opera' from *A Scottish Assembly* by Robert Crawford, published by Chatto & Windus. Used with permission of The Random House Group Limited (p. 61);
- MacNaughton Lord 2000 (extract from *The Story of the Irish Citizen Army* by Seán O'Casey on p. 62);
- Mainstream Publishing ('Eugenesis' from *In Through the Head* by William McIlvanney, pp. 66–67);
- Faber and Faber ('The Horses' from *Collected Poems* by Edwin Muir, pp. 72-73).

Leckie & Leckie would like to thank the following for permission to reproduce their copyright material without charge:
- The Herald Newspaper and Sunday Herald (articles on pp. 11, 13-14 & 16-17);
- Ideal World Productions (image on p. 19);
- Muriel Gray (article on pp. 19–20);
- The Orkney Museum, Tankerness House (image on p. 72);
- The Literary Trustees of Walter de la Mare and the Society of Authors (extract from 'Silver' on pp. 58 & 59);
- Bloodaxe Books (image on p. 69);
- HarperCollins Publishers (book cover image on p. 85);
- HarperCollins Publishers (quotation on p. 86 from *Fahrenheit 451* © 1953 Ray Bradbury);
- Penguin Books (book cover image on p. 102).

Introduction

Welcome to this guide to English at National Qualification Higher level. It is designed to help you, the candidate, prepare and practise for your assessments during the course of the year and, in particular, to develop the skills you will need for the external examination in May.

The importance of English to your future career cannot be overstated. Go into any school in Scotland and you will almost certainly find that the English Department is the biggest department in the building. Why? Quite simply it is because English is needed to pursue any career beyond the school gates: whether it is banking or journalism; science or social work; solicitor or actor; builder or baker – a pass in English, and the communication skills it involves, is an essential requirement.

But English is also about more than planning your career. The study of literature develops our awareness of the world around us. It helps us think about issues and become aware of our own views on topics such as war, poverty and scientific progress. It enriches our lives.

So as well as helping you to prepare for assessments, this book will also assist you to gain as much as is practicable from your English studies, in the widest sense possible. Where exam practice has been offered, for example, there is often advice for further independent study to encourage you in the process of active learning.

Scottish writers have been highlighted in the examples used and I hope you find their stance on various issues stimulating. Their universal concerns are indicative of how literature need know no boundaries.

⟨···· Note

I hope you find the book useful in pursuing your studies and I wish you good fortune in your efforts. But, remember, the only place where success comes before work is in the dictionary!

Larry Flanagan

The study of a Scottish text is compulsory although there is no specific assessment task linked to this requirement

Course and Assessment Outline

There are three units to be studied (each allocated 40 hours of classroom study). A mixture of internal and external assessment applies:

1. **Language**
    Internal   Writing: You must produce a piece of writing under controlled conditions that will be assessed by your teacher as an end-of-unit assessment. Controlled conditions mean that at different stages you need to submit a title, plan, notes and various drafts of the writing in order that the teacher is certain of its validity as your work.

    Close Reading: You need to pass a close reading NAB for Unit Assessment.

    Note ····>

    External   Close Reading constitutes Paper 1 in the external examination. Two thematically linked passages are used at Higher. There are 50 marks and this represents 50% of the total examination mark.

2. **Literature**
    Internal   You need to pass (50% or more) a Textual Analysis Paper for the Unit Assessment.

    External   In the exam, you will attempt two critical essay assignments as Paper 2. These are marked out of 25 and form a total of 50% of the examination mark.

3. **Personal Study**
    Internal   You must produce a critical essay (or spoken response) on a prepared text and task of your own choosing. You write your essay under controlled conditions in one hour, using a maximum of two A4 pages of notes.

NAB = National Assessment Bank: test materials that have been prepared by the SQA for use in unit assessments.

SQA = Scottish Qualifications Authority. This is the body that sets and marks the National Qualifications. It has a very useful website at www.sqa.org.uk that students can access to gain valuable information about their courses.

Language

- Close Reading
- Writing

Language

Making an inference is understanding something that is being suggested or hinted at in a text without it being explicitly stated.

Introduction

Close reading is an area you should be familiar with from Standard Grade. At Higher level you need to show your ability to read and appreciate the detail and content of a text. You should build upon the work you did at Credit and General level, where your close reading skills will have been refined. At Credit level in particular you will have made inferences from a text and sought to understand ideas and arguments as well as specific details in a passage. The Higher requirements for close reading develop these areas further.

←···· Note

There is nothing particularly new in the requirements at this level. However, the balance of the questions alters slightly: there are fewer basic comprehension questions and more attention to an appreciation of the writer's craft and an evaluation of his/her effectiveness.

You will have to pass an internal end-of-unit assessment (NAB) and tackle an external close reading examination, both of which follow the same format.

Purpose of the Assessment

The essential purpose of the assessment is to test your ability to comprehend the meaning and language of a chosen passage. This will involve demonstrating an appreciation of not only what the writer is saying but also how it is being said.

Nature of the Assessment

In an assessment you will have to answer a series of questions on one or two passages. For both NAB unit assessments and the examination, the questions will cover three specific areas of close reading: understanding, analysis and evaluation.

Questions aimed at testing *understanding* will require answers that reveal an understanding of the passage's key ideas. You will be expected to identify important details and explain the main points of the text.

Analysis questions will require you to explain aspects of the passage's structure and style. You will need to examine how the language contributes to the meaning and impact of the writing. Put more simply, this means looking, for example, at how the choice of a particular word might make the meaning clearer or how the writer's use of commas affects the meaning of a sentence.

Purpose and stance are important concepts in writing. Purpose refers to the intention of the writer (e.g. to inform the reader, to persuade, to argue, to explore). Stance is about whether the writer has a particular slant on the topic (e.g. writing from personal experience, believing passionately in a viewpoint, being entirely neutral).

Critical terminology is studied throughout this book and a guide is included in Appendix A (see page 106).

Evaluation questions require you to assess the effectiveness of a text, bearing in mind the purpose and stance of the writer. In this area, use of critical terminology is required and relevant evidence from the text must be used to support answers.

←···· Note

In the close reading examination, two passages will be set. This allows for assessment of your ability to *compare* the issues, style and authorial perspective (purpose and stance) of the texts. An accurate indication of similarities and/or differences is expected in answers.

How to Tackle

Note ····⟩

It is important that you give sufficient time to reading the passage(s). The obvious key to passing a close reading examination is to understand the text(s). Passages will have been chosen because they are of sufficient complexity and depth to require you to read them carefully.

This will mean two readings of the passage. If one reading was all that was required, there would be little test of your abilities.

During the first read, you should pay particular attention to the topic sentences. Topic sentences contain the key messages in a passage and provide the text with structure. (You should be familiar with the role of topic sentences from your own writing!)

Note ····⟩

This should be followed by a look at the questions. The questions asked are an indicator of the important points within the passage.

Then re-read the passage before beginning to answer the questions.

In the Higher examination, where there are two passages, skim read both passages to get a flavour of the paper then re-read passage 1 carefully and tackle the questions on passage 1. Next, re-read passage 2 and do the second set of questions followed by the comparison questions on both passages.

Pay attention to the marks offered – they are an indication of the length of answer required. If there are two marks, for example, you can expect to be either making two points, or making one point and then explaining it in more detail.

Note ····⟩

Answer as directly as you can. Full sentences are rarely required and you should not waste time repeating the question in your answer. 'Quote' means that you can lift the answer straight from the passage. Never miss out this type of question – if in doubt, guess! 'Using your own words', however, is an instruction and straight 'lifts' from the passage will score zero.

Be clear about what the questions are asking. After each one there will be a letter indicating which skill area the question is testing. Make sure that your answer corresponds to the nature of the question.

Understanding questions are concerned primarily with the meaning of the passage – what is being said by the writer.

Analysis questions are more focused on how something is being said. These questions about language are often badly tackled because students do not respond to the actual question. For these questions, you need to focus on the use of language (e.g. tone, the use of metaphor or simile, the order of the words within the sentence). These types of questions are not as difficult as they might seem.

Evaluation is perhaps the most difficult area for many students. Questions here require you to have a holistic appreciation of the purpose and stance of the writer and within this context you have to judge the quality of the actual writing.

Note ····⟩

It is useful to familiarise yourself with the type of passages you may come across in the exam. The simplest way to do this is to regularly read articles from good quality newspapers. Sunday papers (for example *The Sunday Times*, *The Sunday Herald* and *Scotland on Sunday*) are often the best and the magazine sections contain many well-written pieces that will help 'train' your mind.

For more about topic sentences, see the writing section (on page 46).

Where a question is worth a high number of marks (4–6 marks) you might find it helpful to write in short parapgraphs to be sure that you are developing your answer sufficiently to gain marks

Holistic means having a sense of what the writer has been trying to do overall in the whole passage.

Although this is a subjective area, you have to justify your answer by reference to the text. It is essential, therefore, to link any comment and inference made to evidence from the passage.

Think about how the marks on offer might be gained, as this will help you understand the nature of the answer to be given. For example, is a four-mark question looking for two points well made, or four brief points, or one key idea explored at length? Marks must be earned, so ensure your answer is appropriate to the value of the question.

Comparison questions are a combination of both analysis and evaluation but will be focused on the differences and/or similarities between the passages. These may relate to the main point of the passages or to the writers' style or stance. It is important to remember that in working through the rest of the questions you will have done much of the groundwork for this type of question. By the time you tackle these questions, which are always at the end, you should have a clear idea as to what the passages mean.

Be sure to read the introduction to passages as they will indicate the source of the text and, as well as aiding understanding they might help with questions on both passages, e.g. style, tone, purpose

⟵···· **Note**

Close Reading Practice

Some practice passages are provided for you on the next few pages. Begin with the shorter assignments, which are slightly easier, and build up to the Higher-style tasks. Marking guides are provided at the end of this section to allow you to check your work. Try to understand how the correct answers were arrived at. In particular, the marking guide for Passage C has an additional detailed commentary to help you understand how the answers were arrived at (see pages 32–36). After you have tackled that passage, you should study this section carefully.

(Matt Groening/Famous Images)

A   **The following is taken from a Sunday newspaper magazine and is concerned with the changing nature of our language. This passage is much easier than a Higher paper, but it will introduce you to the type of skills required in close reading, particularly in relation to understanding.**

It's official: big hair is worn by ladies who lunch.

After adding Girl Power to their list of words, the *Oxford English Dictionary* has included big hair, ladies who lunch and bikini line to their latest update of the best-selling tome.

5   Big hair, made famous by the likes of Marge Simpson, Destiny's Child and Sarah Jessica Parker, has passed the stringent five-year test to make it into the new edition of the online version of the dictionary. John Breckenridge Ellis first used the phrase in his book, *Lahoma*, in 1913 and style bible *Vogue* described big hair as 'in' last year.

10   Around 50 researchers and language experts constantly collect evidence of the new words appearing in the English language, adding to the collection of hundreds of thousands of words available on the internet. Since March 2000 more than 10,000 words have been added or revised.

America is also being added for the first time as a concept rather than a
15   country, meaning 'a place one longs to reach; an ultimate or idealised destination or aim, an object of personal ambition or desire'.

Other words making it into the dictionary from across the Atlantic include B-Boy, freak, class action and favoured talk-show phrase, tough love – 'the protection of a person's welfare by enforcing certain constraints on him or
20   her'.

Claire Pemberton of OED Online said the dictionary was careful only to include words which had been thoroughly researched and that would stay in use for a prolonged time.

'We collect evidence of words over five years. We have researchers looking at
25   newspapers, books and the internet as well as radio and TV from around the world. We have to have written evidence that the word is going to stick around before we include it.'

There are also some very British entries with blokie, blokeish and big girl's blouse making the cut for the first time. Other British entries include ready
30   meal, social exclusion and drive time, reflecting lifestyle changes in the UK that have made it into the national consciousness.

Pemberton added that the online version would continue to grow for some time.

'We update the OED online every quarter, usually with around 1000 new and
35   revised entries, as part of a 20-year revision plan. It is always evolving.'

Jenifer Johnston   Note ···⟩

If you are interested in finding out more about this topic the web address is www.oed.com

Questions

1. a) What tone is being used in the opening sentence of the article (line 1)? 1A

   b) Show how the writer develops this tone in the phrase 'best-selling tome' (line 4). 2A

2. Explain the writer's use of inverted commas for the word 'in' (line 9). 1A

3. Consider lines 10–13.
   What evidence is offered to support the seriousness of the dictionary project? 2U

4. Why do you think it is the online version of the dictionary that is being updated? 1U

5. 'concept rather than a country' (lines 14–15)
   What is the difference being suggested here? 2U

6. Read lines 28–31.
   Explain one of the lifestyle changes suggested by one of the new British entries. 2U

7. How does the context of the final paragraph support the meaning of the word 'evolving' (lines 34–35)? 2U

8. How successful has the writer been in capturing the reader's attention in this article? 2E

[15 marks]

Please see pages 30–43 for answer guides to close reading passages.

⬅⋯ Note

Tone refers to the attitude being displayed. The context will help you decipher the tone being used. Try imagining the words being spoken – how would they sound? Some words that might describe tone are ironic, sarcastic, friendly, blunt, formal / informal, arrogant, nostalgic, regretful, angry, enthusiastic etc.

⬅⋯ Note

B   **This passage is also taken from a Sunday newspaper magazine.**

Andrea Pearson, *Sunday Herald Magazine***, 9 June 2002**

Walk right in

*They may not have en-suite bathrooms or mini-bars, but youth hostels can offer
other delights. Like steaming hot tea and views to swell your heart. You'll be hard
pressed to find a warmer welcome and you don't have to be a youth to get in.*

I am perched on a cliff ledge under a small but perfectly formed Scots pine
looking into the River Dee raging past below me. It's a good spot to be
perched. There's no evidence of man, just tree, rocks and big, big water.
Anywhere you might care to go in Scotland, in any shire you pick, you can
5   find such places. But that doesn't mean that each time it isn't equally
magnificent. And this is Scotland at its best.

A few yards behind me is the Inverey youth hostel, a simple and rustic affair,
and I have arrived hoping to find a small bunch of bearded men with fleece
tops steaming up the kitchen with a brew and exchanging walking tips. And
10   I would throw my rucksack down and chip in with things like, 'You know a
banana contains all the nutrients you need in the hills,' or 'For me the Brasher
boot still leaves others standing'.

But when I roll up to the Inverey hostel I am greeted by a little notice
informing me it will be open at 1700 hours. It's 1500 hours so I find myself
15   wondering through the birch wood behind the hostel towards the river. To
discover what else might be on offer in this part of Royal Deeside, I head into
Braemar for a drink until the hotels start serving evening meals.

I settle on one hotel described in a guide as having good food in an 'intimate'
setting. However, I am the only person in a large dining room, listening to
20   orchestrated hits from the Seventies. It's raining outside and despite trying to
start the occasional chat with the staff, I am left entirely to my own devices.
It's a bleak supper.

Thankfully, when I pitch up at the hostel, I am welcomed in like an old friend
and there they are – the fleeced folk gathered in the kitchen. A cuppa is served
25   immediately along with a selection of rock cakes – courtesy of Carol and
David Roberts, a retired couple who volunteer for the Scottish Youth Hostel
Association. I am given a quick tour of the hostel which has a men's
dormitory, a women's, an overflow dormitory, and a tiny room in the eaves
which could sleep two.

30   On its door, David has scribbled a sign reading: 'Honeymoon suite, no hanky
panky.' Outside, there are two toilets with cold water sinks. It's bracing, but

Carol always has hot water on the stove for those wanting a hot drink or a wash. David and Carol come here every year and spend two weeks at Inverey enjoying the hills and the birds and feeding hostellers with rock cakes – and

5   it is this volunteering that ensures some of the more remote hostels can stay open to visitors.

The third person in the small kitchen is walking his way from Land's End to John O'Groats for a children's charity and announces he has just had the best day's walk of the whole trip – no small accolade when you consider he has to

40   cross 50 Ordnance Survey maps on his journey. A soggy cyclist arrives and reveals he has completed the same route, but by bike.

And he is only ten Munros short of half way through the magical 284 target. I am starting to feel a little outclassed and wondering if anyone will sniff me out as an impostor. What's this? Only 20 Munros? And you've never walked

45   the length of Britain? What kind of lily-livered sap are you?

Two hardened hikers enter, one is only five Munros short of the lot. Now I am really in trouble. They're going to suss me out very soon. I throw in the banana comment. There are murmurs of agreement, the long-distance hiker always walks with bananas. Wouldn't dream of eating anything else. Yes. I'm

50   in, I've made it. I'm a real youth hosteller.

Throughout the evening we forget each other's names but chat away like old pals. We have at least one thing in common. We love the hills, the wildlife, the peace, the quiet and the massive open spaces that only Scotland can offer.

And most hostellers return again and again to find these things. By breakfast

55   I am feeling inspired. Not just by the other guests, but by David and Carol whose friendliness and love of the outdoors encourages me to head up a high path of some kind. Carol recommends the walk up the Morrone, a hill beside Braemar, as she and David have walked it many times, and she tells me which birds to look out for.

60   Just as we are saying our final good-byes, David rushes out and asks if anyone has left a tenner under the mattress. There are concerned looks all round as no one knows anything about any tenners. 'Well there's still time,' chuckles David as he heads back with a wave.

A youth hostel may not have a plush tartan carpet, a mini-bar or en-suite

65   facilities, but at the end of the day I'd rather have a warm welcome than a warm shower.

N.B. A Munro is a mountain over 3,000 feet. There are 284 of them in Scotland and many hillwalkers see this as a target to be achieved.

←···· **Note**

If you are interested in finding out more about this topic the web address is www.syha.org.uk

Questions

1. How does the writer create a sense of drama in the opening three sentences of the passage (lines 1–3)?   2A

2. Comment on the writer's use of 'But' and 'And' at the beginning of the final two sentences in paragraph one (lines 5–6).   2A

3. Why does the writer use the word 'rustic' (line 7) to describe the hostel?   1A

4. Consider lines 8–9.
   What perception of youth hostels does the writer seem to have?   1U

5. The writer finds herself 'wondering' (line 15) through the birch woods rather than wandering. What does her unusual choice of word convey about how she is feeling?   1U

6. Explain the contrast highlighted in the fourth paragraph (lines 18–22).   2U

7. Consider lines 23–27.
   What is the atmosphere in the youth hostel and how is it conveyed?   2A

8. Explain the meaning of the word 'bracing' (line 31).   1U

9. Re-read lines 37–40.
   How does the writer suggest that the distance from Land's End to John O'Groats is a large one?   1A

10. Show how, in lines 43–45, the writer uses word choice and sentence structure to convey her apparent unease about her inexperience as a hillwalker/ hosteller?   3A

11. 'head up a high path of some kind' (lines 56–57)
    Explain the full meaning of this expression.   2U

12. How effective is the final paragraph (lines 64–66) as a conclusion to the article?   2E

[20 marks]

Getty Images

C **Read the passage below and then tackle the questions on your own as a self-assessment exercise. After that, study the worked model answers on pages 32–36. The passage is moving towards Higher.**

Parable of Wasted Talents
Women still suffer discrimination in the workplace

There are more women than men in Scotland (52% to 48%). Women account for roughly half the Scottish workforce. More than one-third of MSPs are female. Half of Scotland's teachers are women. More than three-quarters of all NHS employees are women. Yet these statistics hide a depressing story about
5   women's prospects of career advancement that is revealed by a hitherto unpublished Scottish Executive report. It confirms that the glass ceiling is still all too painfully and frustratingly in place. The survey of 39 professional bodies carried out by the Executive's Central Research Unit found that women are under-represented at senior levels across all professions, in public and
10   private sector alike.

Equally worryingly, the findings show that many of the bodies (whose responsibilities include representing their members, regardless of gender) were paying, at best, lip-service to equal opportunities issues.

While changing social attitudes, equal opportunities legislation, and
15   economic circumstances have enabled women to make progress in the jobs market, they can still go only so far before banging their heads against the old obstacle. In education, for instance, less than 10% of heads are women, despite equal numbers of female and male teachers. It is not only in the professions where women are getting a raw deal. Women in less skilled jobs
20   are also finding it hard going. Even in lower paid, lower status jobs, women earn on average less than 80% of men's wages. A recent Cabinet Office Women's Unit report on incomes found that, across Britain, the average unskilled woman forgoes nearly £200,000 in a lifetime, rising to nearly £250,000 for women with mid-level qualifications. Highly-skilled women lose
25   nearly £143,000 because of the gender pay gap. Despite equal pay legislation, it appears that large numbers of women are working for less than they should.

The 'mother gap' (the impact on lifetime earnings by taking time off to have children) also militates against women. Many more women than men have to
30   reconcile the conflicting demands of the workplace and the family. Frequently, the only way to do so is to take part-time work (which the statistics prove many women do). It is virtually impossible to make career progress from a part-time base. On the other hand, many women who choose to work full-time are not helped (indeed, might be hindered) by insufficient
35   childcare provision, particularly in private-sector companies. On the basis of its findings, the Scottish Executive unit warns that equal opportunities policies are in danger of losing impact. That is a bleak as well as a worrying conclusion.

We like to think that deep-seated social Scottish attitudes about women
40   (destined for marriage, making homes, and having children) and work (the preserve of bread-winning men) have gone. Although matters have improved greatly, old prejudices and cultural attitudes still persist (as the unit's report confirms). Much needs to be done to change them. There is no easy answer to the matter of child-bearing except a more enlightened and long-term attitude
45   by employers. There is evidence that more women are putting off starting a family until they have a secure base from which to get on when they return to

work. Does this strategy pay off or do women return to their desks only to find that they have slipped down the pecking order while they were away? Some women decide not to have children because they do not want to put
50   their careers at risk. They should not have to face such a choice.

It is not just women who are losing out. The private and public sectors would surely be better run if they had more able and intelligent managers in senior positions. What kind of economic system are we running when, as a matter of routine, talented people are prevented from fulfilling their potential simply
55   because of their gender? There are still too many managers who believe women must adapt to the unbending rules of the workplace rather than the workplace adapting to the needs of women. So much for Britain as a meritocracy.

Questions

1. '52% to 48%' (line 1)
   What is the writer's purpose in using this statistic in the opening sentence?   1A

2. How is the point made in the first sentence developed in the next four sentences (lines 1–4)?   1A

3. Explain the function of the word 'yet' (line 4) in the structure of the paragraph's argument.   2A

4. a) What point is made about 'women's prospects of career advancement' (line 5)?   1U

   b) Show how the writer's word choice in lines 4–10 makes clear his/her attitude to this.   2A

5. What is meant by paying 'lip-service' (line 13)?   1U

6. Read lines 14–15.
   In your own words explain the factors that have allowed women to make progress in the job market.   3U

7. 'banging their heads against the old obstacle' (lines 16–17)
   Comment on the writer's style and purpose in this expression.   2A

8. Read lines 20–25.
   What might be considered surprising about the figures on earnings lost by women in different types of jobs?   1U

9. Explain the use of inverted commas for the phrase 'mother gap' (line 28).   1A

10. How does the context of the sentence support the meaning of the word 'reconcile' (line 30)?   2U

11. What barriers do women who choose to work full-time face in the private sector?   2U

12. Explain the writer's attitude to the conclusion that 'equal opportunities policies are in danger of losing impact' (lines 36–37).   2U

13. Which phrase/expression means the same as 'deep-seated social Scottish attitudes' (line 39)?   1U

14. Consider the use of brackets in lines 40–43. Explain the different functions.   2A

15. What are two of the consequences of the prevailing attitudes to 'child-bearing' (line 44)?   2U

16. How effective has the writer been in presenting an opinionated case?
    Consider two of the following features:
    - the use of parenthesis
    - the use of statistics
    - sentence structure
    - word choice.   4E

    [30 marks]

‹···· **Note**

In sentence structure questions consider whether the sentence builds up to a climax or whether it makes it key point at the start and then exemplifies it. Pay attention to the length of the sentence and the use of punctuation within it. Make sure you understand the use of different punctuation marks: colons, semi-colons, dashes, quotation marks etc.

‹···· **Note**

The 'link' question – when you are answering a question about linkage you need to identify how the word /phrase referred to links back to what has been said and also forward to what is going to be said. Do not write in generalities however – deal with the specific ideas/content of the passage.

D In this slightly abridged article, Muriel Gray rejoices at living in a fast-changing and exciting world and looks forward to a thrilling future for mankind. [Andi is the name that was given to the first genetically modified monkey.] This passage is pitched at Higher standard.

Note ----->

Muriel Gray is a television and radio broadcaster, a journalist and a writer. She lives in Glasgow with her family. Her novels (*The Ancient*, *Furnace* and *The Trickster*) are in the horror/suspense genre and her work has drawn praise from all quarters, including that most famous of horror writers, Stephen King.

Long live Andi the monkey, our ancestor of the future

Nothing will ever be the same again. Does that sentence frighten you? If so, why? Even since you read them a split second ago, the words have proved to be true. Nothing will ever be the same as they were during the moment that you read them. A person who fails to acknowledge this first year philosophy
5 undergraduate truth, that the very essence of life is change, is a self-deluding person, and we, of all the generations who have gone before, should know it better than most.

It's been the most astonishing, mind-boggling privilege to have lived through such a truncated period in history where our youth consisted of a world with
10 few private cars on the roads, two-channel black-and-white television sets considered a perk of the middle classes, no jet travel and no computers. In our recent living memory there was no way to record our voices except on huge reel-to-reel tapes, no way to listen to music except on massive boxes with an arm and needle to scrape over plastic. There was no IVF, no transplant
15 surgery, no microchip technology, no faxes, internet or mobile phones, no greenhouse gases or torn ozone layer. And all this changed while we stood and watched. No other generation in the entire history of our species has experienced such biblically scaled changes within their lifetime, and yet through it all we have remained concerned, thoughtful and deeply interested
20 in morality.

This is important. It's important because whether we like it or not, an unstoppable and inevitable change is about to begin that will make all the previous technological advances seem piffling. Andi, the first genetically altered primate, is the tangible herald of something that has been forecast for
25 decades. As everything from Leonardo da Vinci's helicopter designs to Arthur C Clarke's bombs in space has proved, if we can dream it we can do it. We dream about designing, modifying, changing and improving ourselves, and now it seems we can make it happen.

The one certainty in this whole issue is that it is already too late to stop it. This
30 is quite simply the next stage in human evolution. Whatever pressure groups and politics decide, the science will go on regardless. This is not just idle speculation. This is merely the observation of history. The issue we have to consider is how we deal with the coming transition from old-style take-your-chance humans, and the tweaked, altered and improved future generations of
35 developed world children that will eventually become the norm.

In reality, the moral implications in such a world are no more problematic or complex than they are in the current one. There are worries concerning how we may treat unmodified, 'imperfect' future children in this unknown future. Why? Such meddling already takes place in a primitive way. Right now we
40 do everything we can, using every trick that modern science can muster, to prevent damaged children being born. We try and repair debilitating faults while they're still in the womb, we give the mothers break-through preventative medicine, we transplant, operate, transfuse blood, you name it. But despite it all, when some that can't be helped are still born with terrible

45 handicaps, society dictates quite correctly that we look after them and cherish them. Would this change? That's unlikely while love still exists.

And what about the economic disparity between the wealthy countries and the Third World? What would be the implications in an economic climate where the children of the West would be expensively engineered to be
50 healthy, clever, and long-lived, whereas the Third World remained full of undernourished, poverty stricken people with short, hard, unhealthy lives? Golly. How very different from now that would be.

The most fundamental truth is that there is nothing in the universe that is 'unnatural'. Unnatural is impossible. If man makes it, be it a wicker basket or
55 an atomic bomb, it is a natural thing in the same way a bird's nest or a beaver's dam is. Therefore we have to regard the advance of human intelligence, hypothesis and consciousness as nothing more than an evolutionary tool, and any alterations made to man's environment and himself as a result of that intelligence is as natural as learning to plant and
60 grow was compared to hunting and gathering.

As a species, homo sapiens' days are most definitely numbered on this planet we have managed to temporarily cripple, but since in the history of the Earth we're no more than a tiny blip, why that realisation of our imminent demise should bother us is quite peculiar. The thought of being replaced by
65 something quite different fills some of us not with horror, but with massive optimistic excitement.

Hooray for Andi the monkey. Hooray for change. Hooray for the thrilling enigma of life.

If you are interested in this topic, try watching the 1997 movie *Gattaca*, which portrays a world in which some of these ideas have become reality.

←---- Note

Questions

1. a) Quote the words from paragraph 1 that summarise the 'undergraduate truth' (line 5) referred to. 1U

    b) In your own words explain what this means. 2U

2. 'It's been the most astonishing, mind-boggling privilege...' (line 8)
    Comment on the tone of this line. 1A

3. How does the writer convey a sense of dramatic change in lines 8–16? 3A

4. Explain how the final sentence of the second paragraph (lines 17–20) creates an effective link with the third paragraph. 2A

5. 'the tangible herald of something that has been forecast for decades' (lines 24–25)
    What does the writer mean here? 1U

6. What can you infer about Leonardo da Vinci's 'helicopter' (line 25) or Arthur C Clarke's 'bombs' (line 26) from the context of the sentence in which they appear? 2U

7. Why does the writer believe that genetic science will continue? 1U

8. Why is the word 'imperfect' (line 38) in inverted commas? 1A

9. Explain fully why the writer believes that the moral implications of genetic science will not present a problem in the future. 1U

10. Consider lines 48–52.
    How does the tone of the two sentences contained within these lines help support the writer's meaning? 2A

11. Read lines 53–60.
    Outline the stages of the writer's argument as presented in this paragraph. 4U

12. How effectively does the imagery contained in lines 61–64 convey the writer's view of homo sapiens' role on Earth? 4A/E

13. Explain how the final paragraph, lines 67–68, links in tone and content to the end of the previous paragraph. 2A

14. Muriel Gray is regarded as a lively writer who often presents her readers with an alternative view of topics in the public eye. Considering the passage as a whole, and taking account of the writer's use of language and tone, how effective do you feel she has been in conveying her viewpoint? 3E

[30 marks]

(Jay Freis)/Getty Images

E **Read the following extract from an article by Jason Oddy in which he explores the science of cryonics as a means of achieving everlasting life. Answer the questions that follow. A comparison question (Q14) has been included, which links back to the article 'Long live Andi the monkey, our ancestor of the future' on pages 19–20. The articles would not be as long if two passages were being used in an exam situation. This paper represents a full Higher standard assessment.**

Cool Customers

There is no more forlorn or solitary way to spend a day than being in a room with a group of deep-frozen people. I come to realise this after passing a number of hours with 37 of them in a warehouse on the outskirts of Detroit. Because they are stored in curious white capsules known as cryostats, you
5   can't actually see them. But the longer you spend in their company, the more they succeed in making their chill presence felt. It's not exactly the bodies that create this mournful effect. Instead it's that, in this place consecrated to arresting time and making sure that nothing ever happens, it slowly dawns on you how intolerably monotonous eternity must be.

10 As the Cryonics Institute's sole technician, Andy Zawacki is responsible for keeping the cryostats topped up with liquid nitrogen. He does the rounds once every few days to ensure that his 'patients' remain at a constant minus 196°C. The rest of his time is divided between maintaining the place and manning the institute's adjoining office, which appears to be untroubled by
15 visitors or phone calls. Zawacki must have one of the loneliest jobs in the world.

I've come to Detroit hoping to meet his boss, Robert Ettinger, a now-retired Michigan chemistry teacher, whose book *The Prospect of Immortality* effectively launched the cryonics movement 40 years ago. Today the octogenarian
20 pioneer is apparently stuck at home, so instead Zawacki and I set off on a tour of the premises that starts in the Institute's operating theatre. This is where the journey also begins for aspirant cryonauts who upon deanimating (no one dies in cryonics circles), will be immediately chilled and brought to this room. Here they will undergo a procedure known as perfusion, in which their blood
25 is replaced by a solution that helps minimise the damage that freezing inflicts on body tissue. Next, they are placed in an icebox where their temperature is gradually reduced, until, after a couple of weeks, they are deemed cold enough to be lowered headfirst into a communal cryostat to start their stay in long-term storage.

30 Zawacki built the cryostats himself and he shows off his handiwork with a sort of diffident pride. None of these towering Thermos-style flasks look alike. There is a cylinder equipped with an oddly anthropomorphic protuberance. There are cubes that sport all-over fins. There is even a reclining pod with a fetching domed lid that appears to have come straight
35 out of a Max Ernst painting. It is as though this heterogeneous collection of vessels has, with the connivance of its creator, managed to escape from the realm of strict scientific method into some Hollywood Gothic dream world.

Our tour terminates under the cheerless fluorescent lights of the boardroom, a spot whose most striking feature – whose only feature – is a wall lined with
40 photographs of people who have been cryonically suspended. I can't make the leap between the faces in the pictures and what goes on back in the warehouse. Is it really the case that the nice old man in the straw hat and blue tie is now a rock-solid lump of frigid flesh? And can the auburn-haired

woman smiling gamely beside a fake dwarf Christmas tree truly be stuck feet-
45   up in one of those peculiar vats while she awaits her moment of resurrection?

The basic premise of cryonics is fairly simple. At some point in the future,
medicine will have advanced so far that it will be able to cure every
conceivable ill. Disease, ageing and, of course, that most implacable scourge
of all, death, will all turn out to be reversible. But until that moment arrives,
50   the important thing is to arrest biological time by ensuring that the body, and
in particular the brain, is kept as well preserved as possible.

The great white hope of the cryonics movement is a field of research that's
called nanotechnology. Although only the most fledgling of sciences,
nanotechnology promises one day to be able to construct machines smaller
55   than cells, yet more complex than today's largest computers. And it is hoped
that these machines, or nanobots as they are speculatively known, will –
among myriad other things – be able to repair damaged cellular tissue atom
by atom and molecule by molecule.

According to cryonicists, whose belief in what the future might bring seems
60   altogether unbounded, the most serious threat to everlasting life is the
moment just after you die. Firm in the materialist conviction that the brain,
and the brain alone, is the seat of identity, their greatest concern is that in the
minutes and hours when the blood stops circulating, irreversible structural
damage will be inflicted on this crucial organ. The point of no return they
65   term 'biological death', a state they distinguish from mere clinical death,
which they claim – provided it is caught quickly enough by their elaborate
cooling and perfusion techniques – is just an unavoidable and inconvenient
step on the road to your 'second life cycle'.

Cryonicists freely acknowledge that both freezing and the toxicity of the anti-
70   freeze chemicals will wreak damage on organic tissue. But nanotechnology
allows them to envision a scenario in which trillions of microscopic robotic
surgeons will be released into a frozen body, where they will set about
reversing the molecular damage caused by death, freezing and ageing. Once
cellular health has been fully restored, the patient's temperature will be
75   gradually raised until a blood supply grown from the body's own tissue
begins to circulate. Next the metabolism will be restarted and the cryonaut
will awake to find himself inhabiting a perfectly youthful body.

If this sounds impossibly far-fetched, then apostles of this as yet unproven
science point out that this repairing and replacing of cells at molecular level
80   is something our bodies already do. The difference is that, at present, we do
not have any control over how this process works. Yet with the recent rapid
advances in areas of medicine such as stem-cell research, genetic engineering
and cloning, cryonicists are more convinced than ever that the future is
already knocking at our door…

Jason Oddy

© The Independent October 25, 2002

Questions

1. How does the writer's choice of words in the opening sentence (lines 1–2) convey his feelings?   2A

2. Comment on the use of the word 'consecrated' (line 7) in the final sentence of the opening paragraph.   1A

3. From reading the first paragraph, what conclusion does the writer come to about the possibility of eternal life?   2U

4. Explain the use of inverted commas around the word 'patients' (line 12).   1A

5. What does 'deanimating' (line 22) mean and why has the writer chosen to use this word?   2A

6. Explain what is meant by the final sentence in the fourth paragraph (lines 35–37).   3U

7. Consider lines 38–42.
    How does the writer convey the soulless atmosphere of the boardroom?   2A

8. Read lines 42–45.
    Why does the writer provide details of two of the people in the photographs?   2U

9. How does the writer make the opening sentence of paragraph 6 (line 46) particularly effective?   1E

10. 'The great white hope...' (line 52)
    How does the writer's choice of words in the remainder of the paragraph support the idea contained within this phrase?   2A

Imagery questions – to answer this type of question you must identify the image being used and then relate it to the ideas of the passage. Images are simply pictures/associations created in the reader's mind by the writer's use of language.
Pay particular attention to effective adjectives, adverbs and verbs and to figurative language such as similes, metaphors, personification, etc.

11. What does the writer mean by 'the seat of identity' (line 62)?   2U

12. How effective is the imagery used in lines 70–73?   2E

⟵··· **Note**

13. What does the writer's use of the word 'apostles' (line 78) suggest about his attitude towards the cryonicists?   1A

14. Compare this article with Muriel Gray's 'Andi, the monkey' article.

    a) What might Muriel Gray think about the issue of cryonics?   2U

    b) Comment on similarities and differences between the writers' style and stance.
        Consider such issues as tone, word choice and imagery.   4A

    c) Which article do you prefer and why?   1E

[30 marks]

F   **Passage 1**

Sports shoes have come a long way since the humble plimsoll. In this slightly abridged article Sean Coughlan investigates the rise and runaway success of the trainer.

Sole Legends

In an era of superbrands and mega marketing, trainers have kept their place as a feisty front-runner. They're not just a pair of shoes, but a triumph
5 of the image-makers. They are sports shoes for people who don't play sport, symbols of affluence for people who don't have much money, and urban shoes for suburban kids.
10 They might be packed with plenty of talk about shoe technology, but it's their attitude, not practicality, that sells them. And their image of hip streetwear has a global appeal, with
15 people from Chicago to Shanghai ready to lace up the latest brands. These huge international markets have turned the leading trainer companies into commercial giants.

20 How did these brands become global superstars? Only a few decades ago, sports shoes were still a niche market. Now, the trainer companies are about fashion and
25 lifestyle, selling a whole range of clothes and accessories.

The idea of companies making customised sports shoes began to develop alongside the great surge in
30 interest in athletics and sports in the late 19th Century. In Lancashire in the 1890s, Joseph Foster's company emerged as a specialist shoe manufacturer, producing hand-made
35 running shoes for competitors in the modern Olympic Games, inaugurated in Athens in 1896. This Bolton-based business eventually became the firm that is now known as Reebok.

40 But the types of shoes made by JW Foster and Sons were designed to help athletes run faster, and spiked running shoes were never likely to become a fashion statement. Instead,
45 to find the ancestry of the trainer with street-appeal, you have to look at another humbler type of sports shoe – the plimsoll. This simple canvas and rubber shoe appeared in the second
50 half of the 19th Century, following the development of vulcanisation, which allowed rubber to be bonded more effectively with other materials. And, like trainers, the plimsoll appealed to
55 a wide range of social classes and blurred the boundary between sport and fashion.

For the working classes, the mass-produced plimsoll was an affordable
60 leisure shoe. Day-trippers or Sunday strollers didn't want to be stuck in their heavy working boots, and plimsolls were an attractive summery alternative.

65 For the Victorian middle classes, plimsolls could be worn for any of the summer sports that were becoming popular, whether it was tennis, badminton, cycling or boating, or just
70 promenading along the seafront. And schools adopted the plimsoll as the all-purpose shoe for any kind of physical activity, remaining a basic piece of school kit well into the years
75 after the Second World War.

If the idea of young people playing sport in plimsolls now seems rather quaint, it's a tribute to the powerful marketing of trainers which eclipsed
80 their cheaper and simpler predecessors. In terms of how trainers managed to oust plimsolls from the nation's kitbag, perhaps the key difference was that plimsolls
85 were not a brand. The name was a nickname, applied because people thought the high rubber sole looked like the plimsoll line around the side of a ship.

90 The plimsoll was an easy-to-copy, universal type of shoe but the companies that went on to become the trainer giants were built on the idea of exclusiveness and a strong

95 brand image.

Having established a brand name for a shoe, the great success of the trainer companies was to link this name with the biggest names in

100 sports, a tactic that has been applied again and again. But what really turned this into a global marketing exercise was the arrival of television coverage of sport. Every time a

105 winner went up too collect a medal on the rostrum, the image-conscious shoe companies wanted to see their name in the picture.

Adidas and Puma were pioneers

110 of this showcasing of their products and kept innovating to stay one step ahead. As well as getting medal winners to wear branded shoes, by the 1960s Adidas was producing

115 branded tracksuits, so that people could dress like their sporting heroes.

Big names helped raise the stakes. In the 1970 World Cup, the Brazilian football legend Pele was wearing

120 Puma boots. Adidas could hit back with Muhammad Ali wearing its clothes. It's easy to forget how quickly this branding of clothes spread throughout the sporting

125 world and how quickly it left behind the world of the unbranded, low-cost pair of plimsolls in the duffel bag.

In the 1980s Nike took this marketing style to another level. In

130 any popular history of the 1980s, Nike shoes get a mention, with the "Just do it" advertising slogan becoming part of the language.

It was in this era that the trainer

135 began to emerge as a fashion item in its own right, with the luxury tag fitting in neatly with the decade of "conspicuous consumption". Instead of boasting about how little they had

140 paid for their Oxfam coats, teenagers were boasting about how much more their "box-fresh" trainers had cost.

The different brands each had their own followers, with new types

145 of shoe keeping the customers coming back for more. While fashion was helping fuel the rise and rise of the trainer, the high retail price had to be justified. There had to be a clear

150 difference between the highly expensive trainer and the bargain-basement plimsoll.

Trainer brands have always sold themselves as being innovative,

155 whether it was Puma claiming the first Velcro fasteners in 1968 or Adidas using shark-skin for its sprint shoes in 1972 but from the 1980s, trainers were sold as being a piece of

160 high technology in a shoebox, with all kinds of elaborate claims for the performance-enhancing qualities of soles, heels and uppers. There was "forward thrust" for the sprinting

165 and hi-tech shock absorbers to make the ride more comfortable.

They were marketed as being the product of refined engineering design, almost as if they were car

170 engines rather than running shoes.

In their rise to prominence in the 1980s, they were sold as the living embodiment of energetic living and ambition – footwear for winners in a

175 tough world. As well as being the domain of high-achieving athletes, they were also sold as a symbol of inner-city street fashion, giving trainers a double-edged image.

180 The success of the marketing, pushed on by the rivalry between brands such as Nike and Reebok, was such that, in the 1990s and into the present decade, trainers have

185 expanded into a much wider market. They might be advertised by edgy black teenagers playing basketball in an inner-city parking lot, but they're as likely to be bought by plump

190 white pensioners in Florida.

Trainers have become the footwear equivalent to blue jeans – a kind of global uniform. They've become the everyday shoe for

195 millions of people who never go near an athletic track.

Questions

1. 'They're not just a pair of shoes, but a triumph of the image-makers' (lines 3–5)

   a) What do you understand this sentence to mean?   2U

   b) Explain one of the contrasts used by the writer to support the meaning of this sentence.   2U

2. How does the context help you understand the meaning of the word 'niche'? (lines 20–26)   2A

3. Consider lines 27–57.

   a) What is meant by the phrase, 'specialist shoe manufacturer' (lines 33–34)?   1U

   b) Explain why the type of shoe made by J W Foster and Sons was unlikely to become generally popular?   1U

4. Look at lines 58–75.

   a) Why did the 'plimsoll' become popular?   1U

   b) Explain its appeal to different social classes.   2U

5. a) How effectively does the writer's choice of language in lines 76–89 convey the emergence of the trainer as a superior rival to the plimsoll?   2A

   b) Explain what is meant by 'not a brand' (line 85).   1U

6. Look at lines 96–108.
   What was the key impact of television coverage of sport on trainer companies?   1U

7. Consider lines 109–133.
   How does the writer convey a sense of rivalry between different companies?   2A

8. a) Explain the use of inverted commas around the phrase 'conspicuous consumption' (line 138).   2A

   b) What does this phrase mean?   2U

   c) How does the writer suggest that trainers were part of this scenario?   1A

9. How effective do you find the imagery used in lines 153–170?   4A/E

10. Explain the contrast suggested in lines 180–190.   2U/A

11. How effective do you find the final paragraph (lines 191–196) as a conclusion to the passage?   2E

[30 marks]

Passage 2

In this article Lawrence Michael highlights some of the criticisms levelled at global manufacturers.

Just Sweat It!

Manufacturers of leading brand name trainers – Puma Umbro, Fila Adidas, Reebok, ASICS and Nike – have been beset in recent years by
5 accusations that their expensive products are produced by workers around the world whose rights are being violated and who often have to work excessive overtime for
10 'poverty' wages. The 'sweatshop labour', it is claimed, of people in developing countries is helping to boost the profit margins of these huge global companies.

15 During the 1990s claims of abuse led to many calls for athletes to disassociate themselves from lucrative endorsements with companies accused of exploitative practices and
20 to campaigns for consumer boycotts against the companies perceived as being guilty.

In the run-up to the 2004 Olympics, Oxfam, in conjunction with Labour
25 Behind the Label, published a major report based on interviews with workers producing sports wear and trainers from seven different countries. Long shifts, low wages, job
30 insecurity and a lack of trade union rights were all highlighted as major concerns.

Intense competition between the major companies results in a constant
35 drive to keep prices low and this coupled with the demands of an ever-changing fashion market have resulted, it is claimed, in the suppliers being pressured into minimising
40 production costs – producing the kind of working conditions that have attracted increasing criticism over the last decade.

In response to the allegations most
45 of the major companies have signed up to a variety of ethical agreements, monitoring systems, and 'codes of practice' which, in theory at least, should begin to address the concerns
50 raised by organisations such as Oxfam. In a market that revolves around its healthy lifestyle imagery, negative publicity about the low cost of production in sweatshop
55 conditions is a potential public relations disaster.

Already one manufacturer has tried to steal a march on its competitors by launching a trainer that details on the
60 box the production process involved, all regulated and approved, allowing the caring consumer to achieve a 'guilt-free' purchase. For some it would seem every cloud really does
65 have a silver lining.

Questions

12. Look at lines 1–14.

    a) Explain how the context helps you understand the meaning of 'beset' (line 4) as it is used in the passage. 2U/A

    b) What connection is suggested between 'sweatshop labour' and the 'profit margins' of the global companies? 2U

13. Consider paragraph 2 (lines 15–22).
    What were the two key objectives of campaigners against companies accused of being guilty of 'exploitative practices'? 2U

14. How does the writer's choice of language in paragraph 4 (lines 33–43) support the meaning of the word 'pressured'? 4A

15. What impact does the aside, 'in theory at least' (line 48) have on the meaning and tone of the opening sentence of paragraph 5 (line 44–56)? 2A

16. Explain as fully as you can the nature of the 'potential public relations disaster' (lines 55–56). 2A

17. How effective do you find the final sentence of the passage? 2A/E

[16 marks]

Questions on both passages

18. Explain how the final paragraph of Passage 2 relates to an idea developed in Passage 1. 2U/A

19. Which title do you find more effective and why? 2E

[4 marks]

[Total 50 marks]

Close Reading Answer Section

Passage A - Answer Guide

Model answers are written in this 'handwriting' font.

←···· Note

1. a) *The tone is light-hearted/humorous/tongue-in-cheek.*

    b) *'Best-selling' suggests something popular, whereas 'tome' usually refers to a more heavyweight book that is likely to have less appeal.*

2. *To indicate that it is a colloquial usage, in this case suggesting that big hair was fashionable.*

3. *Over 50 researchers/experts are employed on the project, and with over 10,000 additions, the scale/size of the work suggests it is a serious enterprise.*

4. *Easier to do because books have to be reprinted / Changing a website is less costly.*

5. *'Country' is a literal meaning referring to the geographical location of America, whereas 'concept' refers to ideas that have become associated with America such as The American Dream and home to emigrants from all nations.*

6. *'ready meal' - the idea that we all live busier lives and have less time to prepare and cook a meal so convenience food, ready meals, have become part of our routine.*

    or

    'social exclusion' - a term descriptive of when identifiable groups of people do not share in the wealth or values that most in developed countries do enjoy, and are therefore outside mainstream communities.

    or

    'drive time' - that time of day when working people are heading to and from work largely in their own cars as society increasingly commutes.

7. *'Evolving' suggests gradual, rather than sudden, change. The paragraph talks about quarterly updates, suggesting an ongoing process and the whole project has a timescale of 20 years.*

8. Very effective. The writer has employed an informal tone that suits the topic of new language and she makes a number of modern cultural references, for example, to 'The Simpsons', to interest the reader. Her use of direct quotes from the researcher adds to the effectiveness.

Passage B - Answer Guide

1. 'perched on a cliff ledge' and repeated use of 'perched' - emphasises dangerous situation where fall is possible;

   'raging' - suggests power and danger of fast-flowing river;

   'no evidence of man' and 'just tree, rocks and big, big water' - give sense of isolation, with no-one to help if things go wrong.

2. In both cases the words could have been used without a full stop before them. The writer is deliberately using short sentences to give greater emphasis to each separate idea; the splendour of the scenery and the sense of Scotland at its finest.

3. 'Rustic' describes a rural, countryside location and also a simplicity, an unfussy quality, which both match the hostel.

4. Stereotyped, as she expects to find a particular type of person there: 'bearded men with fleece tops'.

5. It's a play on words suggesting the sense of reflection she feels as she walks through the natural beauty of the woods.

6. The guide used the word 'intimate' suggesting she would find a warm, cosy environment in the hotel; instead it is empty and friendless and she finds it depressing as she sits and eats a 'bleak supper'.

7. Warm and friendly. The use of the colloquial 'cuppa' suggests the informality of the kitchen.

8. 'bracing' suggests sharply refreshing. The idea of washing in the cold water hints at this meaning.

9. She refers to the traveller needing to cross 50 Ordnance Survey maps to complete his journey, meaning he will actually cover the distance detailed on the maps.

10. The words 'outclassed' and 'impostor' convey her unease. 'Outclassed' suggests she feels inferior in some way to the others whilst an 'impostor' is someone who pretends to be what they are not.

The series of questions at the end of paragraph 8 also conveys her unease, as she mocks her own achievements with imagined comments from the others.

11. On one level it refers literally to taking a walk through one of the climbs available in the area but it also refers to the idea that the writer has been inspired to greater things by her stay at the hostel.

12. Very effective. The passage has been about the friendliness of the hostel experience despite its basic provision compared to the plusher surroundings of the hotel dining-room, for example, which, despite its grandeur, was a disappointment to the writer. The repetition of 'warm' as an adjective is effective as it creates the contrast between the 'welcome', which is to do with people, and the 'shower', which is linked to facilities.

Passage C - Answer Guide

1. The brackets here create parenthesis. Using paired commas or two dashes can also do this. The purpose of parenthesis is to provide information that is not strictly required in order for the sentence to make sense but that adds additional information of some kind.

This additional information might be the same idea repeated:

Nicola, the team captain, led the players onto the pitch.

The parenthesis here tells us more about Nicola.

Parenthesis can also be used to allow the author to report a fact but at the same time make a comment (authorial comment) or to make an aside:

Scotland, the unluckiest team in the tournament, was knocked out in the first round.

In the case we are discussing the writer has put in a factual statistic in order to support the general point being made, that there are more women than men in Scotland. So the answer might read:

In order to illustrate the point being made in the first sentence, that there are more women than men in Scotland, in clear, easy-to-understand percentage terms.

2. This is an analysis question so we should be looking at 'how' and not 'what' for our answer.

In each of the sentences the writer gives a statistical example of the role that women play in Scottish society. Our answer then would say:

The point is developed by the writer giving statistical examples of the important role that women play in Scottish society.

Note ····⟩

As this question is only worth one mark you do not need to detail the statistics. If the question had been worth three marks, however, you would be expected to explain each example.

If this was an evaluation question we would be required to give an opinion and to link that opinion to the content of the passage.

This is an effective technique as the repetition of statistics, which show women's prominent role in our society, presents a strong base for the writer to build an argument.

3. The word 'yet' introduces a reservation or qualification, as if something is not fully as we might expect it.

In this case, before the word is used the paragraph produces statistics that at face value suggest women have a significant role in Scottish society. After the word is used we are told that these statistics are not the full picture and that women are not as fully represented in society as might appear to be the case.

Before the word 'yet' is used we are given statistics outlining the role of women in society that appear to be quite positive. However, the tone and content change after the word 'yet' and we are given the more negative view, which is the reality in Scotland.

4. a) This is focused on understanding, i.e. meaning. In this case we can see the writer's use of the word 'depressing' in talking about women's career prospects and there is the clear statement that 'women are under-represented'. These 'clues' give us the answer we are looking for:

Women's career advancement does not happen in the way that it should.

Note ····⟩

In answering this question, we have not simply lifted a quote from the passage as we have not been asked to quote.

b) *The writer uses the words 'depressing', 'painfully' and 'frustratingly' and these suggest that he/she is saddened by this fact/opposed to the prejudice that leads to this situation/disappointed that things are like this.*

Note ····⟩

The marker's instructions are often laid out in this way, as many questions will have more than one acceptable answer. Alternative answers are separated by forward slashes (/).

5. This is an understanding question that simply requires you to explain the phrase. The passage has just stated that women are under-represented and it then states that this happens in some organisations that are supposed to be equal opportunity employers. This is a contradictory state of affairs and if you did not know what lip service meant you should be able to make an intelligent guess from the context that it means saying one thing and doing another.

    Lip service means appearing to say or believe in a thing but your actions show you doing the opposite.

    It is important to look for clues in the text when you are unsure of the meaning of words. Look for connections between ideas – are they similar, opposites, examples, etc?

6. If a question says 'in your own words' and you simply copy a section of the passage you will score zero. Find the key section of the text indicated and then paraphrase it – it is only by using your own words that you reveal your understanding.

Paraphrase = put an expression from the passage into your own words.

⟵···· Note

In this case, you are looking for three points, as there are three marks on offer. The topic sentence of paragraph three lists the three points we are looking for: 'changing social attitudes, equal opportunities legislation, and economic circumstances'. Now put these into your own words:

Different views in society; laws about equal rights; and the financial situation.

3 marks!

7. In this case you are expected to recognise the colloquial use of language, 'banging their heads' – a reference to the saying 'banging your head off a brick wall'. This is linked to the idea of an 'old obstacle', as if things haven't changed.

    The writer employs a colloquial tone in order to suggest the everyday and commonplace nature of the problem facing women.

8. This question asks you to look at the facts presented and draw an inference from them. The answer itself is not stated in the passage – you are required to 'read between the lines'.

    The most surprising feature is that the most highly skilled women are not the biggest losers.

9. Identify which use of inverted commas applies to the example and then explain it using the detail of the passage. You will get no marks for simply identifying a general usage; it must be specifically linked to the text.

Inverted commas are used for specific purposes. They can surround a title, enclose direct speech, mark out a quotation, and indicate when a word is being used in a non-literal sense or is not standard English usage.

⟵···· Note

'Mother-gap' is not in standard English usage. It is a made up word, which is being used as an effective shorthand way of describing an aspect of the issue being described (a fuller explanation is provided in the brackets).

10. Context is simply the words and sentences around the phrase/word referred to in the question. The remainder of the sentence talks about the conflicting demands of home and work. As the paragraph is about women who work and bring up children we can see that reconcile means bringing together two opposite ideas; resolving a conflict.

   Of course if we know what reconcile means it is easier to start with an explanation of the word and then show how the context reveals this. However, even where we do not know what a word means, we can use the context to infer from it what the meaning of a word is, or to allow us to make an intelligent guess.

   Reconcile means to resolve two opposing ideas. The context helps reveal this by talking about the conflicting ideas of 'the workplace and the family'.

11. First locate the key words/phrase, 'insufficient childcare provision', and then put it into your own words. Locating the answer is made easier by the phrase 'particularly in private-sector companies' which relates directly to the question.

   A lack of facilities for looking after children.

12. The sentence that follows this statement contains the words 'bleak' and 'worrying'. The writer's choice of these words conveys a clear viewpoint.

   The writer's attitude is one of concern and also a sense of despair.

13. The question requires nothing more than a straight quotation. Clearly the repetition of the word 'attitudes' acts as a guide for an educated guess.

   'old prejudices and cultural attitudes'

14. The brackets create parenthesis (see Question 1, above). Once this is recognised the task is to see exactly what is being done in each example.

   The first set of brackets gives us detailed examples about the nature of 'deep-seated social Scottish attitudes about women'.

   The second set gives a definition of 'work', which is a further example of the attitudes towards women.

   The third set is an aside, citing a report that supports the point made in the sentence.

15. This is a straightforward understanding question.

Note ⸱⸱⸱⟩

Although this question appears near the end of the paper it is no more difficult than the questions at the beginning. Never, therefore, give up even if you find one or two earlier questions difficult.

Some women are waiting until later to start families in order to establish themselves in their career first, and some are deciding not to have children at all.

16. Questions that require you to evaluate the writer's effectiveness are to some degree open to opinion. Your viewpoint, however, must be supported by reference to the passage. It is permissible to develop a point you may have referred to in another answer.

   Generally speaking, for four marks you would identify, and then explain, two key points from the passage. Sometimes four marks can also be gained by making four separate points clearly.

   The following are examples of acceptable approaches:

   The writer has been very effective in presenting an opinionated view.

   Parenthesis is used on several occasions to provide evidence to support the writer's argument and to indicate the stance taken by the writer. In the fourth paragraph, for example, within brackets it states 'indeed, might be hindered' which puts a stronger emphasis on how the situation works against women. (2 marks)

   The writer makes effective use of statistics to support his/her assertions about the role of women in society. A good example of this is where the actual salary losses are quoted in order to prove the impact of discrimination on women's earnings. (2 marks)

   The writer often uses short, sharp sentences to drive home a particular point. In line 43, for example, it reads 'Much needs to be done to change them.' The use of simple sentences such as this contrasts with the more usual complex sentences of the passage and creates emphasis for the point being made. (2 marks)

   The writer's word choice is also effective in creating a stance. Words such as 'bleak' and 'depressing' clearly indicate the author's viewpoint as essentially disapproving. (1 mark. For two marks, this answer could go on to talk about the words having connotations of being dismal or joyless.)

Connotation is where a word is seen as suggesting particular ideas or images to the reader. It is used a lot in poetry and creative writing.

Denotation is where a word is literally specifying an object.

For example: rose can be taken to denote a particular type of flower but in a given context it can be used to suggest beauty:

'O my Luve's like a red, red rose
That's newly sprung in June...'
Robert Burns (1794)

⟵···· Note

1. a) 'the very essence of life is change'

    b) A central fact of life is that everything is constantly changing.

2. The tone is one of excitement and vitality. The words 'astonishing' and 'mind-boggling' help create this feeling through their connotations and also their slightly colloquial sense of being overpowering.

3. Gray gives detailed examples of things from the past that might now be considered obsolete, starting with items from her youth and then moving to living memory. Then she gives details of things that exist now but did not until quite recently. By comparing the two sets of lists she creates a sharp and dramatic contrast.

4. The final sentence of paragraph 2 highlights the idea of society retaining a sense of values. This idea is referred to in the opening of paragraph 3 by linking the word 'This' and the importance of the idea is developed in the remainder of the paragraph through the challenge it now faces from Andi.

5. This answer requires you to provide a brief explanation of the meaning of the phrase: 'the tangible herald of something that has been forecast for decades'. For example:

    Living proof of the scientific predictions of the past few decades.

6. That they were early proposals for something that eventually happened.

    The context talks about things being dreamt about and then happening, suggesting that the same process applied to da Vinci's helicopter designs and Clarke's space bombs.

7. Because of our previous history and the idea that evolution is inevitable.

8. Because we are not meant to take it literally, as a judgment on the people being described, but rather as a shorthand way of describing human beings with their normal range of faults.

9. Because, despite the theoretical and practical advances in science, we will continue to love our children.

10. Tone is often a difficult concept for students when we are talking about written passages. If we were discussing tone in relation to speech it would be easy to tell when someone was being sarcastic or tongue in cheek or humorous and so on. Tone means the same thing when it is written – we simply have to look for clues in the words used or the context of the passage, instead of hearing them in the spoken voice.

The tone is heavily ironic and it supports Gray's meaning because she is saying that things are that way already.

11. *Everything that exists is natural. Man is a natural creature and therefore anything we make is part of our natural world. As we evolve, we develop greater capacities to alter our environment. Any such changes must themselves be regarded as part of a natural process.*

12. *The writer feels that human beings have not looked after the planet well, in fact we have damaged it. This is suggested by her use of the word 'cripple', with its connotation of injury. She also feels that our role has been short-lived and ultimately not very consequential. This is conveyed by the phrase 'tiny blip', with 'tiny' suggesting our insignificance, as does 'blip', which is little more than a brief dot on a screen.*

13. *The end of paragraph 8 emphasises a positive view of the future and an embracing of the challenges it will bring.*

This positive tone is continued by the use of 'Hooray' three times, one of them being for Andi who is symbolic of the future. The word 'thrilling' is used, also linking with the idea of excitement.

14. Answers should regard the passage as being effective, although any viewpoint sustained by appropriate reference to text and style can be considered legitimate.
Points might include:
- liveliness of writing
- word choice
- power and force of argument.

The expression 'most astonishing, mind-boggling privilege' is a good example of the luridness of the writing style.

The mixture of enthusiastic tone and colloquial choice of language combine to clearly convey her feelings of excitement and involvement.

Her repetition of the word 'Hooray' in the final paragraph echoes this sentiment with its three cheers for Andi, the monkey.

Passage E - Answer Guide

1. Answers should pick up on connotations of 'forlorn' (hopeless) and 'solitary' (lonely/ isolated) to suggest the writer's negative feelings. One mark for each. One mark, also, if suggestion made that 'deep-frozen' relates to sterility of process, lack of emotion, etc.

   The writer's feelings must be explained for full marks.

2. Answers should link the word to religious practice or particular solemnity, appropriate for tomb/mausoleum atmosphere of warehouse.

3. *That it would be unbearably tedious.*

   Gloss on 'intolerably' and 'monotonous'.

   Note ⟶

   'Gloss' is where you take the words of a passage and paraphrase them to reveal your understanding of it.

4. *Non-literal use of the word as a patient is someone being treated for a medical disorder but here it is being used to refer to people who are actually dead, albeit frozen.*

5. *It means stopping living, dying. It's been used because that is the word that cryonicists use to avoid acknowledging death as a finality/reality.*

6. *The variety (heterogeneousness) of containers for the frozen bodies seem to be more than just functional, as they would be on a strictly scientific approach, as they are artistically designed, almost like a film set.*

7. *The word 'cheerless' suggests a cold, unemotional setting. The lack of decoration, 'whose only feature', again suggests a functional rather than comfortable space.*

8. *To present them as individual human beings, thereby emphasising his difficulty in associating these people with the frozen masses inside the containers. It makes the contrast more effective.*

9. *The sentence is short and straightforward, reflecting its content, which suggests cryonics is 'fairly simple'.*

10. *The phrase suggests expectations being raised about something that hasn't happened yet: 'hope'. This is further emphasised by words such as 'fledgling' (beginning/early stages), 'promises' (unfulfilled as yet), 'hoped' (desired in future) and 'speculatively' (gamble).*

    Any two plus gloss on 'great white hope'.

11. *The location in our bodies where each individual's characteristics are defined.*

12. Any sensible comment on 'trillions of microscopic robotic surgeons'. For example:

    The word 'surgeons' is effective in suggesting the idea that nanobots will heal the damage caused by the 'death, freezing and ageing' process. 'Robotic', however, reflects the artificial nature of the process and the word 'trillions' creates a scale that might appear to be frightening, or possibly far-fetched.

13. *'Apostles' usually refers to followers of a religious figure. It's as if he is suggesting that cryonicists see this science as a new religion or belief.*

14. a) *Given her general enthusiasm and acceptance of the advance of science she may very well welcome the possibilities suggested by cryonics.*

    The possibility of her being opposed to cryonics is acceptable, also, if it is linked to the idea in her passage that humans are relatively insignificant in the history of the world and we don't deserve to live forever.

    b) There is no single correct answer to this question. The key, however, is to link your comments to textual evidence from each of the passages. Some areas that might be covered include:
    - Both are written in the first person but also for an audience.
    - Gray is more opinionated and direct in addressing the reader, e.g. 'Does that sentence frighten you?' She is also argumentative in tone.
    - Oddy's personal opinion is understated and revealed through language rather than direct comment, e.g. 'forlorn and solitary' and he is more reflective in tone.
    - Gray is enthusiastic about the science she discusses whilst Oddy seems slightly bemused.
    - Both make effective use of imagery, e.g. 'a tiny blip' (Gray); 'the future is already knocking at our door' (Oddy).

    c) Answer is based on personal choice but a reason for your choice must be given, e.g.

    I prefer Gray's passage because I agree that humans are relatively insignificant in the sweep of the history of the planet.

    I prefer Oddy's article because it provides technical details, which help you decide for yourself if cryonics is a good or bad thing.

Passage F – Answer Guide

Passage 1

1. a) Answers should show an understanding of the fact that trainers are not merely functional items but also fashion icons.

    b) Any one from:

    Sports shoes for people who don't play sport. Symbols of affluence for people who don't have much money. Urban shoes for suburban kids.

    Explained as:

    healthy/competitive aspects of sport for people who don't actually participate in any such activities.

    Indicator of wealth/style for those who might not actually be wealthy.

    Idea of street wise/chic/tough city image for people who live in comfortable residential areas.

2. *'niche' means specialised or narrow area.*

    Context talks of the past, a few decades ago, and contrasts this with 'now' where trainers are about fashion and style, and are 'global' suggesting a change from the past where they were more specialised.

3. a) *That they produced shoes specifically for sporting purposes.*

    b) *Purpose was dedicated to athletic performance; specialised nature e.g. spikes meant they were only practical for that activity.*

4. a) *They had wide appeal and moved beyond only being a sports shoe to general leisure use.*

    b) *Working people found them affordable and a pleasant alternative to their working footwear. The middle classes found them adaptable as they could be used for a wide range of sporting activities.*

5. a) Answers should demonstrate an understanding of how completely the trainer took over from the plimsoll. Good answers will include references to 'eclipsed' and 'oust'. 'Quaint' might be commented on, although such an answer is likely to be weaker.

    b) Plimsoll is a general reference word like trainer – it didn't have individual labels/company names and therefore wasn't marketed in the same way.

6. *It served to create an international market for trainers.*

7. References might include:
   - innovating to stay one step ahead: new developments to keep in front of their rivals
   - example of branded clothes as an 'innovation'
   - raise the stakes: sense of gamble between protagonists
   - specific examples of rival personalities: Pele versus Muhammad Ali
   - 'hit back': sense of conflict.

8. a) *They are being used to create a shorthand title based on a particular pattern of behaviour from that period.*

   b) *The idea that people flaunted their wealth, that people indulged themselves and wanted everyone to be aware, ostentatious behaviour.*

   c) *Because they were seen as fashionable and pricey.*

9. Marks will depend on the quality of comment on selected references. Answers should link trainers to the concept of a high quality engineering product.

   Possible references include:
   - 'high technology in a shoebox'
   - 'performance-enhancing'
   - 'forward thrust'
   - 'hi-tech shock absorbers'
   - 'refined engineering design'
   - car engines rather than running shoes.
   NB Reference alone scores zero marks.

10. Contrast is being used to demonstrate wide appeal of trainers: different ethnic backgrounds; different age groups; different living areas; different levels of fitness.

11. Effective – references should be to 'global uniform', 'everyday shoe for millions'.
    Marks will depend on effectiveness of comment. Reference alone scores zero marks.

Passage 2

12. a) *'Beset' means to be troubled by.*

    The context talks of accusations, using words like 'violated' to create a negative impact. One mark for meaning and one for appropriate link to context.

    b) *That the cheap labour implied by 'sweatshop' is creating bigger profits for the companies.*

13. *To persuade famous athletes to stop promoting some companies. To persuade the public not to buy certain brands.*

14. 'Pressured' means compelled or forced.
    Appropriate references include:
    - 'constant drive'
    - 'demands'
    - 'ever-changing'.

15. *Changes it from being a statement of certainty to one with an element of doubt, suggesting that the companies may not in practice actually adhere to the codes.*

16. *Trainers thrive on their publicity as reflecting healthy lifestyles and a certain style. Being linked to what might be seen as scandalous exploitation will damage that image.*

17. *Effective. It shows how the some companies can turn the situation to their advantage and gain additional customers as a result, with the example of marketing the non-exploitative production methods.*

Questions on both passages

18. *It reveals the intense competition referred to in the first passage and how the companies are always seeking to 'innovate' to stay ahead.*

19. Answer is based on personal choice but a reason for your choice must be given.
    Sole Legends – play on the word sole linked to soul music and references to 'edgy black teenagers'; Legends linked to status of trainers and endorsements from famous sport personalities.
    'Just Sweat It' – play on the Nike slogan 'Just do it' but with pointed link to the idea of sweatshop labour.

Language

Introduction

Writing skills are a key part of the assessment requirements for Higher English. They are tested whenever you write a critical essay in response to literature, and they are also specifically assessed as part of the language unit.

You might choose to write in any of the following genres: argumentative, persuasive, personal/reflective, prose fiction, drama script, poem(s), report.

You should know from Standard Grade what type(s) of essay you are best at and it therefore makes sense that you choose a style of essay that you are already good at for this assignment. The likelihood is that your teacher will ask you to tackle a number of writing tasks during the period of your course, although only one has to achieve a pass mark for the unit assessment.

It is important to understand that by developing your writing skills you are also developing your ability to close-read passages and to respond to literature, as all of these skills interact in a holistic manner.

Purpose of the Assessment

Whatever form of essay you attempt, the assessor will be looking for evidence of your ability to express yourself in a coherent, thoughtful and logical manner. You will be expected to make full use of your vocabulary and reveal your understanding of the normal features of good writing – accurate spelling, sound sentence structures, and effective punctuation.

Nature of the Assessment

You will be required to write an essay, under controlled conditions, for internal assessment. The piece of work must be creative, expressive or a report.

A minimum of 650 words in length is required, except for poetry, although this should be regarded as an absolute minimum for most tasks.

Controlled conditions, in this instance, means that the teacher will require to see at different stages a draft title, an outline plan, a first draft, and then the final piece.

Four performance criteria apply to the essay:

1. Content
    The key areas for you to consider are the relevance of your content for the purpose of your essay and the need for your writing to show a sound, strong development. Clearly, given that this is a National Qualification that you are attempting, some depth to your ideas is expected.

2. Structure
    Structure refers to how you organise your paragraphs and ideas in your essay.

    You will be expected to have an effective and appropriate structure, which assists the content in having impact on the reader. In other words, it will be well organised, be creative where appropriate and it will help make your ideas clear to the reader.

3. Expression
    Expression is about how you say something rather than what you say.

    You will be expected to display an effective choice of words and make use of a variety of sentence structures to create a style to the essay that helps make your meaning clear.

4. Technical Accuracy
    It will be expected that spelling, syntax and punctuation will be consistently accurate.

Note ⋯⋙

Syntax refers to the order of the words in a sentence. This is referred to in more detail on page 47 of this book.

How to Tackle

Specific advice is offered below on writing particular types of essay, but first there are some general points that can be applied to all writing (including your critical essays).

Go for a Good Opening

Get straight to the point of your essay. The marker does not want to wade through a load of waffle. Create a good impression immediately by seizing the marker's attention.

Weak   *I think that our society is faced with a great number of problems.*
Improved   *Society is in a mess.*

A good opening creates impact so avoid beginning with a long-winded sentence (or even paragraph). Short, sharp and to the point is best.

Punctuation

Remember to use punctuation correctly – a series of comma splices in your first paragraph would create the wrong impression!

A comma splice occurs when, instead of putting in a full stop or using a conjunction, the writer attempts to join together two sentences or independent clauses with a comma. For example:

> *John ran downstairs, he was excited and nervous because today was the day his exam results arrived, unfortunately, he failed English because he used too many comma splices.*

This could be rewritten as:

> *John ran downstairs. He was excited and nervous because today was the day his exam results arrived. Fortunately, he passed English because he knew how to use punctuation.*

Using the semi-colon

The semi-colon is a much-underused punctuation mark that could help a number of students avoid the peril of comma splicing! Essentially it is used to join together what could be two separate sentences but where the content is such that the writer wishes to underline the connection. Charles Dickens' opening to *A Tale of Two Cities* is a classic example: *It was the best of times; it was the worst of times.*

Language

Bring a bit of colour to your essay through your choice of language. Use vigorous, vibrant verbs that spring out from the page. Employ adventurous adjectives. Write in the active voice. Say exactly what you mean. Express yourself!

Examples:

Verb: walked (Why would anybody just walk?)
Alternatives: trudged; hobbled; sauntered; strode; plodded; skipped; meandered; traipsed – all of these add more descriptive detail than someone merely walking.

Adjective: Adjectives describe nouns and they enhance your writing by expanding the detail of your description:

The house lay empty.
The neat, freshly painted house lay empty.
The decrepit, ivy-covered house lay empty.
The warm and inviting house lay empty.

In each of these cases the choice of adjective creates a style and tone that supports meaning.

Active voice: Use the active voice for verbs to create directness and pace, which enlivens your writing:
Mary rode her shiny new bike with a sense of pride.

As opposed to the passive voice:
The new bike was being ridden with a sense of pride by Mary.

Figures of Speech

Similes, metaphors and personification are ways of enhancing your writing, adding colour and life to your words. They are particularly important in descriptive and personal essay writing where you are trying to convey a sense of emotion or capture the essence of a scene or place.

The small cottage nestled in the bosom of the hill; its lights twinkling like the sailor's starry sky, guiding my ship safely home to port.

Avoid Clichés

Clichés are overused, worn-out phrases such as 'A game of two halves', 'The teacher's bark was worse than his bite', 'The detective was hot on the trail of the tuck shop thief' and 'A shiver ran down her spine'. They should be avoided.

Paragraphing
Topic Sentences

A paragraph is a group of sentences about the same topic. Paragraphs are the building blocks of a good essay, interlocking together to create a coherent whole.

Good paragraphs normally have good topic sentences. A topic sentence is a statement of the paragraph's main idea. Usually it opens a paragraph, although it can also act as a conclusion.

Developing Your Paragraphs

Good paragraphs develop logically, assisting the reader to follow the extension of the writer's main idea.

Some ways of developing a paragraph:

Details	provide facts or information about a topic
Examples	illustrate a point by giving an example
Comparisons	make your point by comparing two things
Contrasts	consider opposites to highlight a topic
Question and Answer	pose a question and then answer it

Link Your Paragraphs

Paragraphs are not mini-essays. They should be linked together. Some useful transitional words and phrases that can be deployed include: therefore, as a result, nevertheless, furthermore, moreover, rarely, occasionally, often.

Try to present your ideas logically. Events, for example, should be chronological unless you wish to create a particular effect. If you are describing a particular scene consider starting the description from a distance and then gradually get closer, thereby creating a structure to your writing.

Finish Strongly

As with your opening paragraph, the final one is crucial for impressing the marker. Always finish strongly and emphatically. Highlight the importance of any given topic. If you are writing a persuasive essay, for example, make your final viewpoint obvious.

Be Clear about Purpose

Purpose is essential for effective essay writing. Make sure you are fully aware of what you are attempting to do in your essay and use the appropriate register and tone for that purpose.

Remember, it is easier to write about something you know about or have experienced than it is to create a different world. Even where you are writing imaginatively, locating your story in concrete experience will help you sustain your writing.

Note ⸺⤍

Register refers to the use of a group of words that are associated with a certain type of essay or speech. For example words such as 'aforementioned' and 'alibi' would suggest a legal setting whilst 'Dearly beloved' would be appropriate for a Church Minister's funeral oration.

Sentence Structure (Syntax)

Candidates often let themselves down by using a repetitive, pedestrian style in relation to their sentence structures.

Sentences are normally formed around a verb, which is a word or phrase describing the action, and the verb will have a subject (the person or thing doing whatever is being done). The usual sentence structure will have the subject coming first, followed by the verb, and then followed by any additional information being provided.

In close reading you are often asked to comment on the syntax of a sentence, where the writer has altered the normal word order to create a particular effect, perhaps beginning with an adverb to create a particular mood, e.g. 'Quietly, the shadowy figure crept around the room.' You should attempt to do the same in your own writing.

For example, when we join two sentences together we often use a conjunction:

John ran home quickly. He heard his heartbeat.

becomes:

John ran home quickly and he heard his heartbeat.

Another way of achieving this, however, is to take one of the verbs and to turn it into the '–ing' (present participle) form and then to use it as the opening of the sentence:

Running home quickly, John could hear his heartbeat.

This begins to vary our sentence structure and show the marker our ability to manipulate language. In this case we have the bonus of starting the sentence with a verb, which creates a sense of urgency and movement.

This structure also allows us to develop a complex sentence without overusing conjunctions such as 'and'.

> *Running home quickly, John heard his heartbeat and inside himself he felt a sudden surge of life and hope.*

The one thing you need to remember if using this technique is that it can only be achieved when the subject of both verbs is the same. Look at these examples to see what is meant here.

> *Feeling hungry, Keri ate an apple.*

Correct, because Keri is feeling hungry and Keri eats the apple.

> *Climbing the huge apple tree that sat at the bottom of the garden, Bryan felt a warm glow of achievement.*

Correct, because Bryan is climbing the tree and Bryan feels the warm glow of achievement.

> *Opening the envelope, a letter fell out.*

Wrong, because this would mean that the letter opened the envelope and the letter then fell out. In this case the original sentences would have had two different subjects, e.g.

> *Tricia opened the envelope. A letter fell out.*

Try looking over a previous essay to see where you could have improved your writing by combining some sentences in this manner.

Specific Genres – Creative (prose, poetry and drama)

Writing a Short Story

Good short story writing is an area that requires both a level of expertise and some creative flair. Some students will excel in this genre and hopefully everyone will enjoy attempting to be creative.

A short story should have three elements:
- characters
- setting
- plot.

It is important that the characters are more than just names – they should have personalities. Limit the number you use; two or three is normal, four at most. If you can, base them on people you know. (You may wish to change the names however!)

Make sure you use direct speech to give your characters life:

'What do you mean?' asked the confused but desperately keen student.
'I mean, make your characters talk. It livens up your essay and it will get you a higher mark,' replied the wonderfully kind and very clever English teacher.

Note ····⟩

The setting should normally be somewhere reasonably familiar to you. The more familiar you are with the setting the more realistic it will appear in your essay.

The plot has three stages: beginning – middle – end. It will include conflict/dilemma and at the end of the story something will have changed, otherwise nothing has happened! The change does not have to be overly dramatic. It might involve, for example, the main character realising a truth about him/herself or about someone else; it may be that the reader gains an insight into an issue by viewing the world you create in your story; it may be a physical change relating to the setting. However, if at the end of your story everything is the same as it was at the beginning, what has been the point of the story?

It's like saying to someone, 'Wait till I tell you what happened!' And then when you are eagerly pressed for details, you reply, 'Nothing much.'

The early part of your story should be used to establish the characters and the basic scenario. In the middle section you develop the conflict/dilemma and then in the final section you resolve the problem. Note that these are not three equal parts to the essay in terms of length as the early and middle sections will almost certainly be much longer than the ending. However, all three sections are important when writing a successful short story.

When you are attempting to create a character or a particular mood or atmosphere in a short story, it is important that you make full use of your vocabulary and that you demonstrate your ability to manipulate language to your purpose.

If, for example, you are describing a scene, attempt to make the marker feel that he or she is present and can visualise the moment, savour the excitement, enjoy the contentment.

Make use of effective figurative language but avoid hackneyed expressions or over-dramatisation.

Rules for direct speech

1. Speech marks (inverted commas) should be used before and after any words that are actually spoken.

2. Each time there is a change of speaker take a new line, no matter how short the spoken part has been. You can continue a paragraph after direct speech, however, if there is no change of speaker.

3. Begin each new speech with a capital letter.

4. Before closing your speech marks there must be a punctuation mark. If it is the end of the speech and sentence, use a full stop. If it is a question, use a question mark. Where you continue the sentence to indicate who was speaking, use a comma instead of a full stop and then put a full stop at the end of the sentence.

Read the following short prose extract and consider how effectively the writer creates a particular mood and atmosphere in only a few sentences.

Storm Over Glasgow

Like an off-white shroud draped loosely over the corpse, the sky hung over Glasgow's grey streets. Pregnant with heavy rain the grey clouds stretched over the ribs and bones of the city's thoroughfares. The ragged skyline seemed to tear open the veil and torrents gushed forth upon the homes and houses, the parks and pavements, the thousand various denizens that are the city of Glasgow.

Example of a Short Story

Read the following short story. It was written in response to a task that asked the student to end with the words, 'Below, the intruders were gone, but neither the people nor the place would ever be the same again.'

How successful has the writer been in creating a plot, setting, characterisation and deploying effective sentencing and language choice? Some comments are offered at the end of the story.

Intrusion

A cold sun shivered over the horizon as the first of the heavy trucks rumbled down the sand-dust lane towards the village encampment. A clean-shaven young man changed gear with one hand whilst using the other to deftly avoid potholes with swings of the steering wheel. Behind him two rows of jerking green-jacketed torsos stared at the wooden floorboards of the vehicle, shaded from the light by a skin of green canvas pulled tightly over three cold steel ribs.

Some five miles further on Yasha was filling water cans for the breakfast happenings. A group of women clustered close by her, awaiting their chance to turn the tap on the water tank.

Yasha's dog skipped around her heels as she headed home. Laughing, she sprinkled liquid drops on its head to tease the beast. Its yelping only made her laugh more and she had to resist the temptation to empty one of her two buckets over the poor animal. To do so would mean rejoining the queue, at the wrong end. To return home with only one bucket - such a row she could not face so early in the day. Besides water was precious and she would feel guilty about wasting it.

As she thought of the day ahead the convoy snaked its way downhill towards the camp.

Today would be a good day, Yasha decided. She often made such decisions, convinced of her own ability to determine the nature of the world. Sometimes fate coincided with her declarations - today it would not.

The men in uniform entered the camp at precisely 7.45 a.m. on the morning of October 31st. Four hundred and thirty-one deaths later they left.

Women cried in Yasha's home. Their tears mixed with the blood of Yasha's father and that of her eldest brother.

In a shadow by the water tank Yasha huddled her fear around her. The broken body of the dog, shattered by the heavy boot of a green-jacket, lay close by her. 'She's only a child. Leave her be,' a voice had ordered.

Overhead the cold-blue sky was empty of cloud. And the sun shone.

It dazzled the eyes in the stubbled face of the front driver, as the convoy crawled slowly towards the rim of the hill.

Below, the intruders were gone, but neither the people nor the place would ever be the same again.

The plot of the story is clear – an army patrol invades a refugee camp and kills many of the people there before departing. Put as briefly as that the storyline may seem a little thin but in short stories it is the quality of the writing as much as the basic idea that creates the story's success.

In this story our sympathy is drawn to the character of Yasha, a young girl presented to us as a friendly carefree individual who becomes traumatised by the violence she witnesses. Note how this character is portrayed through the way she acts rather than a long descriptive paragraph. Note also the writer's attention to detail – the inclusion of the playful dog in the early part of the story and the reference to its dead body towards the end. Figurative language is used effectively throughout the story to enhance the description, for example, 'a skin of green canvas pulled tightly over three cold steel ribs,' and 'Yasha huddled her fear around her.'

Consider the impact of sentences such as, 'Four hundred and thirty-one deaths later they left.' Why has the writer been so precise with the number of deaths?

Direct speech is used sparingly in this particular piece of writing but it is effective as it reveals how close the central character came to death herself: 'She's only a child. Leave her be,' a voice ordered.

Think about why none of the soldiers have names.

Overall this is a very effective piece of writing that demonstrates the writer's control of language, confidence in sentencing and creative flair.

Poetry

Poetry writing creates its own demands and it is not practicable in this volume to exemplify the many varied ways in which this genre could be tackled.

You can submit a single poem or a series of thematically liked poems.

Poetry, however, should not be regarded as an easy option simply because it is likely to be shorter than other choices. You will need to demonstrate a knowledge and understanding of form and pattern, of poetic techniques such as figurative language, rhythm and rhyme, and you will need to demonstrate an ability to consider a topic or theme in an original and effective manner.

Drama

Writing a dramatic script is an option that may appeal to some candidates, particularly those involved in Drama Studies.

As with short story writing, a certain creative flair is required to create an effective dramatic script and you should be confident in your understanding of the genre.

Clearly there is the need to be able to create effective and believable characters, to establish a setting that allows for dramatic conflict to happen, and to be able to handle the demands of using dialogue to tell and develop a story.

Knowledge of how to lay out a script and to include appropriate stage directions are also essential.

Specific Form – Expressive (persuasive, argumentative and reflective)

Writing an Argumentative or Persuasive Essay

⟸···· **Note**

If you are writing an argumentative or persuasive essay, you will be expected to prepare thoroughly before you begin your actual writing. There is no excuse for inadequate research. The major benefit of research is that you should have an abundance of ideas to help you clarify your thoughts and write your essay.

Remember, however, that you must not simply copy out someone else's work, as this would be heavily penalised – make sure that you acknowledge any sources you use. The SQA has issued advice to candidates on this matter and every attention should be paid to it – plagiarism is unacceptable. Students who are caught plagiarising can be disqualified from all their SQA assessments, not simply the subject where they have been found out.

For persuasive essays the following plan is straightforward, but perfectly adequate.

First, be clear about your viewpoint. Your opinion should be firmly held and expressed in the opening sentence/opening paragraph.

⟸···· **Note**

In an argumentative essay, you will explore various sides of a topic in a more balanced manner, substantiating viewpoints with evidence. In a persuasive essay, you will adopt a particular stance and try to persuade the reader of the validity of your case through force of argument.

Researching information for this type of essay has never been easier. Many publishers now produce "issue books" aimed at teenagers on topical concerns such as racism, drug abuse, the environment, ethics, etc. The internet is also full of sites dedicated to debate and discussion. Remember, however, that the internet can be an unfiltered source of opinion and you should not simply accept as truth everything you find there. A good site to get you thinking is www.debatabase.com

General plan:

Paragraph 1   Statement of attitude – state your subject and make clear your stance.

Paragraph 2   Argument 1   Present the first point in support of your position and then develop the paragraph.

Paragraph 3   Argument 2   Repeat this procedure for your second point, preferably using a different approach to developing your topic.

Paragraph 4   Argument 3   As for paragraphs 2 and 3.

Paragraph 5   Refutation of opposite viewpoint – here you should introduce an argument that might be used against your view and refute it. Having stated the idea clearly, you should then counter it with an appropriate response. (What you are doing here is demonstrating confidence in your own position by taking account of other points of view. This in turn allows the reader to understand that you have thought both about and around a subject.)

Paragraph 6   Restatement of attitude – finish by strongly reiterating your opening point of view, and possibly drawing on some of your argument to underline your position.

A longer essay would simply incorporate more paragraphs into the general approach outlined.

You may wish to write a more complex argumentative essay, perhaps balancing two conflicting viewpoints or exploring a range of views on a topic without supporting any particular stance personally, i.e. writing objectively.

The approach is not dissimilar. For a balanced essay, the following plan is a useful structure:

Paragraph 1   Introduce your subject and indicate some of the main issues you intend to discuss.

Paragraph 2   Side 1   Introduce an aspect of the subject and then outline the main argument that might be used to support it and comment on/evaluate the issue.

Paragraph 3   Side 1   Introduce a second aspect of the subject, again outline the main argument that might be used to support it and comment on/evaluate the issue.

Paragraph 4   Side 2   Introduce an opposite aspect of the subject, then outline the main argument that might be used to support it and comment on/evaluate the issue.

Paragraph 5   Side 2   Introduce a further aspect of the subject from the opposite viewpoint, again outline the main argument that might be used to support it and comment on/evaluate the issue.

Paragraph 6   Interface the contrary viewpoints and try to balance the weight of evidence used to support the differing views. Arrive at a conclusion, which does not necessarily need to be in favour of either side of the argument.

Example of an Argumentative/Persuasive Essay

Consider the following topic sentence plan – can you see how it lays the basis for a sound persuasive essay?

Why I support the legalisation of euthanasia

Euthanasia is an idea whose time has finally come. [Refer to growing levels of support.]

First and foremost euthanasia is about our rights as human beings. [Develop argument on right to choose.]

Euthanasia is also about the right to dignity in death. [Illustrate with case study.]

Aside from the individual arguments in support of legalisation, there is the significant potential advantage to society in terms of released resources in an already overstretched NHS. [Use facts and figures about cost of terminal care.]

Why is the UK so slow in following the lead of other countries? [Compare situation here with somewhere like the Netherlands; consider safeguards built in.]

Some people object to euthanasia on moral and religious grounds. However … [Answer the religious argument – not compulsory.]

In conclusion, … [Sum up key points again.]

Writing a Personal/Reflective Essay

This is a popular essay format and has the benefit of being based on your own experiences. However, the most common mistake made is for candidates to simply retell the story of a particular event. Such an approach will not achieve a good mark.

You must reflect on your experience. Try to express your thoughts and feelings as clearly as you can and show how the experience has affected you. Convey to the reader a clear sense of your own personal involvement and reveal any insights that you may have gained.

Write sensitively about yourself, allowing your personality to sparkle through your words. This can be helped by using descriptive language, such as adjectives and adverbs, and by making use of similes and metaphors in order to explain/explore your feelings.

What the marker is looking for in particular is a sense of how the experience has contributed in some way to your development as a person. You should not write what might be termed a descriptive essay. Many students write about very personal experiences for this option and there is an understandable concentration on the specific detail of the incident or memory – the death or funeral of someone who was very close to you, for example. To achieve the highest mark, however, you need to show a level of mature reflection and perspective on the event being described and a degree of insight into the experience.

Above all, be genuine in your thoughts, feelings and reactions.

It is difficult to exemplify this type of essay without writing a full personal piece, but the short paragraphs below give a flavour of the tone and style that would be appropriate in a reflective piece.

Example 1

Looking back at those events I can see how childish and immature I was but at the time my actions seemed so justified. It's odd how even a few years can change your perspective. Back then my father was so in the wrong and I was so in the right. Now, perhaps, we would both agree that it wasn't so clear cut.

Example 2

I can be quite a difficult person to get along with because I demand perfection in everything and sometimes you just cannot expect that. It took a particularly embarrassing experience for me to realise that however…

Specific Form – Report

Writing a Report

Report writing differs from argumentative/persuasive writing in that you are attempting to present complex information in a non-personal, objective fashion.

Firstly, you must agree with your teacher the topic and focus of your report. This will be expressed in a statement of the report's purpose. Once this is done you will need to collate information from a variety of sources and then present it in essay form. The minimum number of sources must be four, and these can be from a wide range of categories such as articles, surveys, maps, television, databases, etc. Your statement should indicate the intended resources.

In terms of collating information a few simple steps apply:

Use the agreed purpose of your task to plan your notes. For example, imagine you have chosen to write a report on racism in Scottish society. To focus your task you might decide to define the nature of racism; consider the impact it has on society and individuals; and outline the steps that are been taken to tackle the problem. (Whatever your topic, the essay requires to have a logical structure to it.)

Each of these aspects will help you focus information into different sections of your report. Write each at the head of a separate piece of paper and then consider the information from your sources.

Likely sources for this essay might include a Commission for Racial Equality leaflet; a school's Equal Opportunities policy; a newspaper clipping about a racist incident, with quotations from the victim; statistics on racially motivated crimes; an information leaflet from the Scottish Executive.

As you read through the sources highlight or note the key points made and list them under the appropriate heading from you task. Try to put the points into your own words at this stage as this will help you avoid copying in your final essay.

A few tips to remember:
- Where you come across statistics, concentrate on the point being made by the information rather than the bald figures.
- Anecdotes (personal experiences/stories) are useful to illustrate an aspect of a situation but it is the point that is being made that you should concentrate on for your notes not the details of the story.
- Similarly, when you are given a list of examples, focus on what they are examples of rather than the examples themselves.

Once you have made your notes you need to re-organise the information you have gathered as it will be in the random order that you read the sources. Look to see the connections between different items of information as this will help you create cohesive paragraphs when you start writing.

Writing the report

A report should be written as far as possible in formal prose. This means you avoid shortcuts such as contracting words (Don't!); you do not use quotations or colloquialisms; and you are not required to use figurative language to give your writing a creative flourish. Present the information as you have found it and try to keep you own personal opinion out of the essay. The primary purpose of your report is to inform the reader – not to persuade him or her, although you are allowed to draw a conclusion based on the information you have presented.

In your report, you may use diagrams, charts and graphs if they are required by the topic and you can use headings and bullet points to organise information. This is particularly useful if your report draws upon work you are doing in a different subject, which is permitted as long as the general rules about independent work are adhered to – your English teacher would be the final judge on that.

Writing a Report

Stage 1
Task – create a specific task for your report e.g.
An examination of racism in Scottish Society.

Stage 2
Establish the key areas of focus, e.g.
Definition of racism and indication of its scale in Scottish society.
The problems caused by racist behaviour for individuals and for society.
Steps being taken to tackle the issue.

⟵···· **Note**

Three or four specific areas should be sufficient for you to write a reasonably sustained piece – remember these are not paragraphs but sections of your essay.

Stage 3
Identify and read your source material, highlighting key points from the texts.

Stage 4
Collate your key points under the different sections of your rubric, linking related material where appropriate.

Stage 5
Write the report, using your own words and acknowledging the sources you have consulted at the end in a bibliography .

Literature

- Textual Analysis
- Critical Essay

Literature

Introduction

Textual analysis is about you responding critically to an unseen piece of literature. It assesses the same skill areas as the critical essay, but in a different way. In textual analysis you will be asked specific questions on a given text rather than be asked to write an extended essay.

Textual analysis on an unseen text is a compulsory assessment for your unit pass in Literature, but it is not part of the external examination.

Purpose of the Assessment

Textual analysis, as with the critical essay, is concerned with your ability to respond thoughtfully to a literary text, be it a poem or an extract from a play or prose work. The NAB test is designed to show if you have understood the writer's purpose, if you appreciate the writer's craft and if you can demonstrate a genuinely personal response to the text.

Nature of the Assessment

You will be asked a series of questions on a given text or extract, designed to test your abilities in the following areas:

Understanding	This refers to your ability to demonstrate your understanding of the main concerns and significant details of the text(s) studied.
Analysis	Here you are expected to explain ways in which aspects of structure help convey meaning. You will also need to examine how the language and style of the extract contribute to its meaning and impact.
Evaluation	This is where you show that you have thought about what the writer is saying, how he/she is saying it and have in some way engaged with the ideas in the text.

How to Tackle

Essentially, *understanding* questions are about what is being said by the writer, *analysis* is about how it is being said, and *evaluation* is about how well it is being done.

You need to be clear about the type of question being asked in order to ensure that your answer is effective.

Consider the following short extract from a poem and the practice questions that follow.

Silver

Slowly, silently, now the moon
Walks the night in her silver shoon:
This way, and that, she peers, and sees
Silver fruit upon silver trees . . .

Walter de la Mare

Q What is the content of the scene described in this extract?
A In considering the scene's content, you would talk about the poet's description of moonlight casting a silvery light over the scene.

Q How does the poet's use of language help create a clear picture for the reader?
A In discussing this, you could talk about the alliteration on the letter S throughout the verse; the personification of the moon as an inquisitive traveller; the repetition of the word 'silver'; or the use of commas in line 3 to create pauses mimicking the action of someone looking this way and that.

Q To what extent has the poet been effective in conveying the atmosphere of the scene described?
A To evaluate how effective the description is, you could discuss how the idea of 'silently' is appropriate to suggest the quiet of night or the slightly spooky atmosphere of the silvery scene; you might say that personification of the moon is effectively sustained through the verbs 'walks', 'peers' and 'sees'; you could explain how the repetition of silver gives tone and colour to the poem.

Note ···▷

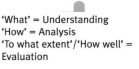

'What' = Understanding
'How' = Analysis
'To what extent'/'How well' = Evaluation

In dealing with textual analysis, it is important to be able to use the correct terminology for particular aspects of language such as the use of similes and metaphors. A guide to technical terms is included in Appendix A (see page 106).

When you are reading a text, think all the time about its meaning and any inferences you can draw from it. You should highlight any features you notice in preparation for answering the questions.

For example, the extract on the previous page might have looked like this after your first reading:

Silver

Slowly, silently, now the moon
Walks the night in her silver shoon:
This way, and that, she peers, and sees
Silver fruit upon silver trees . . .

Walter de la Mare

Try the practice papers provided before working through the guided marking scheme. The first of the texts is designed to introduce you to textual analysis and then they get gradually more difficult, allowing you to develop your skills as you practise. The poems used in E, F and G are quite substantial, longer than you will face in a timed assessment. You may wish to pursue further study of them, however, with a view to their potential use in critical essay responses. Their inclusion here underlines the fact that the analytical skills required for textual analysis and for critical essay are essentially the same – both assess your ability to respond to literature.

(Crispian Woodgate/Getty Images)

Philip Larkin is regarded as one of the major English poets of the 20th century. He was born in 1922 and received many awards in recognition of his writing before dying from cancer in 1985. You can find out more about this poet at www.philiplarkin.com, home of The Philip Larkin Society.

Textual Analysis Practice

Textual Analysis Practice Paper A

←···Note

Wires

1 The widest prairies have electric fences,
   For though old cattle know they must not stray,
   Young steers are always scenting purer water
   Not here but anywhere. Beyond the wires

5 Leads them to blunder up against the wires
   Whose muscle-shredding violence gives no quarter.
   Young steers become old cattle from that day,
   Electric limits to their widest senses.

Philip Larkin

Questions

1. Consider the first line of the poem.
   How is an apparent contrast suggested by the poet?   (2)

2. Briefly explain why the 'old cattle' might 'know they must not stray'.   (2)

3. Look at line 4.
   a) How effective do you find the expression, 'Not here but anywhere'?   (2)

   b) 'Beyond the wires'
      Comment on the location of this phrase within the structure of the poem.   (2)

4. Look at lines 5 and 6.
   By commenting on imagery and language, explain how the poet views the
   young steers' experience with the electric fences.   (4)

5. Look at lines 7 and 8.
   a) What does the poet see as the consequence of this experience?   (1)

   b) How does the poet's word choice in the final line help suggest that the
      cattle are not simply physically enclosed?   (3)

6. This is a poem about experience. Explain the wider significance of the poet's
   theme and comment on how effective you think the poet has been.   (4)

[20 marks]

Please see pages 74–82
for answer guides to
textual analysis passages

←··· Note

Note ⋯⟶

Singer sewing machines were very popular home sewing machines in the sixties. Here the poet recalls his experience as a young boy of watching his mother work away on such a machine.

Robert Crawford is a Professor of English at St Andrews University. He was born in 1959 in Bellshill and attended school in nearby Glasgow. You can find out more about him at his website:
www.st-andrews.ac.uk/academic/english/crawford/home.html

Opera

1   Throw all your stagey chandeliers in wheelbarrows and
move them north
To celebrate my mother's sewing machine
And her beneath an eighty-watt bulb, pedalling
5   iambs on an antique metal footplate
Powering the needle through its regular lines,
Doing her work. To me as a young boy
That was her typewriter. I'd watch
Her hands and feet in unison, or read
10 Between her calves the wrought-iron letters:
SINGER. Mass-produced polished wood and metal,
It was a powerful instrument. I stared
Hard at its brilliant needle's eye that purred
And shone at night: and then each morning after
15 I went to work at school, wearing her songs.

Robert Crawford

Questions

1. Look at lines 1–4.
   a) Explain the contrast created in the early part of the poem between the 'stagey chandeliers' and the 'eighty-watt bulb'. (4)

   b) What does this contrast suggest about his mother's situation? (1)

   c) Quote a word that indicates the poet's attitude to his mother's work. What does it tell us? (2)

2. How do we know that the poet felt a sense of awe watching his mother work? (2)

3. The poet compares his mother's sewing machine to a typewriter, a machine that he as a writer might use. In what way might the two be similar? What is the reader meant to understand about the poet's attitude towards his mother's work, by this comparison? (3)

4. 'stared hard' (lines 12–13)
   What do these words suggest about the effect of the sewing machine on the poet as a young boy? (2)

5. Why does the poet use a colon in the second last line? (2)

6. a) Explain how the poet develops the image of music in the last 4 lines. (3)

   b) How does this link with the title of the poem? Why has he chosen this title? (2)

7. How effective has the poet been in conveying the feelings behind this childhood memory? (4)

[25 marks]

For more information about the
Irish writer Seán O'Casey, visit
the following website:
www.rte.ie/millennia/people/
ocaseysean.html

The Irish Citizen Army lined up in front of Liberty Hall
with a crowd of onlookers.

Textual Analysis Practice Paper C

⟵···· Note

The Story of the Irish Citizen Army

*(In this descriptive extract, the Irish writer Seán O'Casey gives a stirring first-hand
account of a meeting of Dublin workers in the early part of the twentieth century.
They are on strike against their employers and about to form a Citizens' Army to
help them win their campaign.)*

Discontent had lighted a blazing camp-fire in Dublin. The ruddy light of the
flame was reflected by an earnest and ominous glow in the face of every
Dublin worker. Men, full of the fire of battle, thronged in dense masses the
wide, expansive area facing Liberty Hall. The city was surging with a passion
5 full, daring, and fiercely expectant; a passion strange, enjoyable, which it had
never felt before with such intensity and emotion. It was felt, unconsciously,
that this struggle would be the Irish Armageddon between Capital and
Labour. The workers were exuberantly confident that the unparalleled spread
of the sympathetic strike would overthrow the moneyed hosts of Midiam.
10 Did you not hear it? It was true, many great scholars had declared in their
favour, and even now Captain White, the aristocrat and gentleman, was with
their beloved Leader, and had signified his intention to throw in his lot with
his socially humbler brothers, abandoning the privileges of position, ignoring
the remonstrances of friends, choosing freely and bravely to stand by the
15 people now in their hour of need.

And the eager, toil-worn, care-lined faces of the workers now turned with
concentrated uneasy patience towards the window on the left-hand side of
Liberty Hall, waiting for it to be raised, that they might listen to this nightly
message of hope, progress and encouragement from those Leaders, whom
20 they were convinced would guide them safely through the heavy ordeal that
each man must share that there might be preserved to all the elemental right
of the workers to choose their Union, and to follow the Leaders in whom
alone they placed their whole confidence and trust.

The disappearing Artist Sun had boldly brushed the skies with bold hues of
25 orange and crimson, and delicate shades of yellow and green, bordered with
dusky shadows of darkening blue, which seemed to symbolise the glow of
determination, the delicate hues of hope, and the bordering shades of restless
anxiety that coloured the hearts and thoughts of the waiting, watching masses
of men that stood silently beneath the oriental-coloured panoply of the sky.

30 Suddenly the window is raised...

⟵···· Note

'Midiam' (line 9) is a biblical
reference.
It suggests that the workers saw
their employers as brutal
outsiders.

Questions

1. Look at the first three sentences (lines 1–4).
   What is the mood of the workers and how does the writer suggest this to the reader? (4)

2. a) What effect is gained by the repetition of the word 'passion' (lines 4–5)? (1)

   b) How does the writer develop different meanings for the word? (2)

3. 'exuberantly confident' (line 8)
   How does the word 'exuberantly' add to our understanding of the workers' mood? (1)

4. 'socially humbler brothers' (line 13)
   Quote an earlier phrase about Captain White that confirms the class distinction between the men and him. (1)

5. 'abandoning the privileges of position, ignoring the remonstrances of friends, choosing freely and bravely to stand by the people now in their hour of need.' (lines 13–15)
   How does the structure of this extract support the image of Captain White as a man of action and determination? (2)

6. The tone of the second paragraph is more sombre than that of the first. Which two expressions in particular contribute to this heavier mood? Explain your choices. (4)

7. How effective has the writer been in the third paragraph in both capturing the detail of the sunset and also reflecting the mood of the crowd of waiting workers? (4)

8. Do you feel that the final short paragraph acts as an effective conclusion to this extract? Explain your answer. (1)

[20 marks]

Norman MacCaig was born in Edinburgh in 1910 and he grew up there, attending the Royal High School and then Edinburgh University. During the Second World War he was a 'conscientious objector'. MacCaig is studied in many Scottish schools and his work is often noted for its dry sense of humour and wit. He died in 1996.

Textual Analysis Practice Paper D

In this poem the Scottish poet Norman MacCaig writes about his impressions on a visit to New York City.

⟵···· Note

Hotel room, 12th floor

This morning I watched from here
a helicopter skirting like a damaged insect
the Empire State Building, that
jumbo size dentist's drill, and landing
5   on the roof of the PanAm skyscraper.
But now midnight has come in
from foreign places. Its uncivilised darkness
is shot at by a million lit windows, all
ups and acrosses

10   But midnight is not
so easily defeated. I lie in bed, between
a radio and a television set, and hear
the widest of warhoops continually ululating through
the glittering canyons and gulches –
15   police cars and ambulances racing
to the broken bones, the harsh screaming
from coldwater flats, the blood
glazed on sidewalks.

The frontier is never
20   somewhere else. And no stockades
can keep the midnight out.
                    Norman MacCaig

Sample Highlighting

As you read through a textual analysis passage, highlight key words, phrases and figurative language as a first stage in your response to the text. For example:

Hotel Room, 12th Floor

This morning I watched from here   *personal narration*
a helicopter skirting like a damaged insect   *simile*
the Empire State Building, that
metaphor jumbo size dentist's drill, and landing
5   on the roof of the PanAm skyscraper.
change But now midnight has come in   *personification*
from foreign places. Its uncivilised darkness   *key words*
metaphor is shot at by a million lit windows, all
ups and acrosses   *imagery*

Questions

1. What effect is created by the brevity of the title? (1)

2. Consider lines 1–6
   The poet does not appear to be overly impressed with the view of New York. Comment on how his use of language and imagery in these lines convey this impression. (4)

3. Consider lines 6–9.
   a) Explain the change signalled by the use of the word 'But' in line 6? (2)

   b) How does the poet suggest that 'darkness' is a threat? (4)

   c) 'is shot at by a million lit windows'
      How effective do you find the poet's word choice and use of imagery in this line? (4)

4. Look at lines 10–12: 'between a radio and a television set'
   Why does the poet make this reference? (2)

5. Consider lines 13–15
   The poet links the scenes in the city to the history of the American Wild West? Comment on two of the ways in which he does this. (4)

6. Consider lines 16–19
   Explain as fully as you can how the poet's word choice suggests the violence of the city? (4)

7. Consider the final stanza of the poem.
   a) What is the poet referring to when he talks about a frontier and what does he mean when he says 'the frontier is never somewhere else'? (3)

   b) How effective do you find this stanza as a conclusion to the poem? (2)

[30 marks]

William McIlvanney is a widely respected Scottish writer. He is perhaps better known as a novelist with books such as *Docherty*, *The Big Man* (made into a film starring Liam Neeson and Billy Connolly), and his three 'detective genre' novels, *Laidlaw*, *The Papers of Tony Veitch* and *Strange Loyalties*. His characters often reflect McIlvanney's strong sense of social justice. You may be interested in reading one of his books for your personal study text. To find out more about McIlvanney check the following website, which is maintained by The Association for Scottish Literary Studies – www.arts.gla.ac.uk/ScotLit/ASL S/ Laverock-McIlvanney-1.html

Textual Analysis Practice Paper E

Consider the poem below and then tackle the questions that follow. When attempting a textual analysis, particularly of poetry, you should first read the text straight through to gain an overall impression of it. On your second reading, highlight any striking or unusual aspects you discover: for example, use of similes or metaphors, techniques such as alliteration, key images and so on. After thinking about the poem yourself, read over the questions as they will clearly direct you to the key ideas and techniques of the writer. By having thought about the text yourself, you will be better prepared to answer the questions.

Remember, you may change your mind about your initial impression as your understanding of the text deepens.

The first two stanzas have been reproduced after the poem, with some points highlighted for you, by way of example. You do not need to identify or comment on every single feature. What you are trying to do is get a feel for the text.

In this poem, William McIlvanney speculates on what our future world might be like.

N.B. Eugenics is the science of racial purification. Genesis is the first book of the Bible. It tells the Judaeo-Christian story of creation, describing how God fashioned the world in six days and then rested on the seventh.

⟵⋯ Note

Eugenesis

On the first day they eradicated war.
Nations were neutralized. In desert places
The cumbered void rusted with defused bombs,
The gutted chambers. In random heaps
5   The rockets lay, like molar monuments
To brontosauri sentenced to extinction.

On the second day They fed the starving.
The capsules gave immunity from hunger.
Faces filled. The smiles were uniform.
10   The computers had found a formula for plenty.

The third day ended work. With summer
Processed to a permanence, the sun-
Machine in operation, every day
Would be as long as They desired it.
15   Season-chambers were erected. The nostalgic
Could take a holiday to autumn if they wished.
The computers thought of everything.

On the fourth day death was dead.
Synthetic hearts, machine-tooled brains,
20   Eyes and limbs were all expendable.
Immortality came wrapped in polythene.
Every face was God's you saw upon the street.

By the fifth day crime was cured.
Mind-mechanics, They located every hatred,
25   Extracted it, and amputated angers.
Each idea was sterilized before its issue.
The computers fixed a safety-mark for thinking.

The sixth day saw heaven's inauguration.
Benignity pills were issued. Kindness meetings
30   Were held on every corner. They declared
Love as the prerogative of all.
That day became the longest there had been.
But as long as there was light the people smiled.

On the seventh day, while They were resting
35   A small man with red hair had disappeared.
A museum missed a tent. Neither was found.
He left an immortal wife, the changeless years
Of endless happiness, and a strange note
In ancient script, just four historic letters.
40   The Autotongue translated: 'Irrational Anger.'
The Medic Machine advised: 'Rejection Symptoms.
Source Unknown. Primordial and Contagious.'

It was too late. The word ran like a rash
On walls and daubed on doorways. Cities emptied.
45   In panic They neglected Their machines.
The sunset was unauthorized. Its beauty
Triggered the light-oriented metal cocks
That crew until their mechanisms burst.
Fires twinkled in the new night, shaping mattocks.
50   On the dark hills an unheavenly sound was heard.
The Historometer intoned into the silence:
'Ancient Barbaric Custom Known as Laughter.'
Seizing up, the computers began to cry.
                                William McIlvanney

Sample Highlighting

Eugenesis

On the first day they eradicated war.   *who?*
Nations were neutralized. In desert places *alliteration, abrupt statement*
The cumbered void rusted with defused bombs, *image of decay*
The gutted chambers. In random heaps
The rockets lay, like molar monuments
To brontosauri sentenced to extinction. *unusual simile*

On the second day They fed the starving. *change to capital letter*
The capsules gave immunity from hunger. *like curing a disease?*
Faces filled. The smiles were uniform. *sense of order?*
The computers had found a formula for plenty. *scientific progress?*

Questions

1. Explain the simile used in the first verse (lines 4–6). How effective do you consider it to be? (3)

2. From the second verse onwards 'They' has a capital letter. Why has the writer chosen to make this change? (1)

3. What does the poet mean by the following lines:
'The computers had found a formula for plenty.' (line 10)
'Immortality came wrapped in polythene.' (line 21) (4)

4. 'machine-tooled brains' (line 19)
'Each idea was sterilized before its issue.
The computers fixed a safety-mark for thinking.' (lines 26–27)
   a) How does the poet's word choice here suggest a more sinister aspect to this apparently perfect world of the future? (4)

   b) What is it that concerns him most? (1)

5. 'the changeless years of endless happiness' (lines 37–38)
How does this expression imply dissatisfaction? (2)

6. Detail the stages of the 'rebellion' (lines 35–53). (3)

7. What might the 'four historic letters' be (line 39)? (1)

8. What is symbolic about the crowing of the metal cocks (lines 47–48)? (1)

9. Explain the irony of the last line. (2)

10. Consider the structure of the poem. Events begin on the first day and continue through to the seventh. Explain the parallel being drawn here and why it is appropriate. (2)

11. What do you consider the poet's main message to be and how effective has he been in conveying this viewpoint to the reader? (6)

[30 marks]

Jackie Kay is a modern Scottish writer. She is black and her work often explores issues of identity, as in this poem. Ibo is the name of one of Nigeria's largest ethnic groupings, some 15 million strong.

Note ····⟶

Jackie Kay was adopted by a white Glaswegian couple. In *The Adoption Papers* she explores in some detail her own life story. You may also be interested in reading her novel *Trumpet* or her short story collection, *Why Don't You Stop Talking*. She also has a further poetry anthology entitled, *Off Colour*. To read an interview with Jackie Kay, visit: www.randomhouse.com/ boldtype/0499/kay

Pride

When I looked up, the black man was there,
staring into my face,
as if he had always been there,
as if he and I went a long way back.
5   He looked into the dark pool of my eyes
as the train slid out of Euston.
For a long time this went on
the stranger and I looking at each other,
a look that was like something being given
10   from one to the other.

My whole childhood, I'm quite sure,
passed before him, the worst things
I've ever done, the biggest lies I've ever told.
And he was a little boy on a red dust road.
15   He stared into the dark depth of me,
and then he spoke:
'Ibo,' he said. 'Ibo, definitely.'
Our train rushed through the dark.
'You are an Ibo!' he said, thumping the table.
20   My coffee jumped and spilled.
Several sleeping people woke.
The night train boasted and whistled
through the English countryside,
past unwritten stops in the blackness.

25   'That nose is an Ibo nose.
Those teeth are Ibo teeth,' the stranger said,
his voice getting louder and louder.
I had no doubt, from the way he said it,
that Ibo noses are the best noses in the world,
30   that Ibo teeth are perfect pearls.
People were walking down the trembling aisle
to come and look
as the night rain babbled against the window.
There was a moment when
35   my whole face changed into a map,
and the stranger on the train
located even the name
of my village in Nigeria
in the lower part of my jaw.

40   I told him what I heard was my father's name.
Okafor. He told me what it meant,
something stunning,
something so apt and astonishing.

Tell me, I asked the black man on the train
45   who was himself transforming,
at roughly the same speed as the train,
and could have been
at any stop, my brother, my father as a young man,
or any member of my large clan,
50   Tell me about the Ibos.
His face had a look
I've seen on a MacLachlan, a MacDonnell, a MacLeod,
the most startling thing, pride,
a quality of being certain.
55   Now that I know you are an Ibo, we will eat.
He produced a spicy meat patty,
ripping it into two.
Tell me about the Ibos.
'The Ibos are small in stature
60   Not tall like the Yoruba or Hausa.
The Ibos are clever, reliable,
dependable, faithful, true.
The Ibos should be running Nigeria.
There would be none of this corruption.'

65   And what, I asked, are the Ibos' faults?
I smiled my newly acquired Ibo smile,
flashed my gleaming Ibo teeth.
The train grabbed at a bend,
'Faults? No faults. Not a single one.'

70   'If you went back,' he said brightening,
'The whole village would come out for you.
Massive celebrations. Definitely.
Definitely,' he opened his arms wide.
'The eldest grandchild – fantastic welcome.
75   If the grandparents are alive.'

I saw myself arriving
the hot dust, the red road,
the trees heavy with other fruits,
the bright things, the flowers.
80   I saw myself watching
the old people dance towards me
dressed up for me in happy prints.
And I found my feet.
I started to dance.
85   I danced a dance I never knew I knew.
Words and sounds fell out of my mouth like seeds.
I astonished myself.
My grandmother was like me exactly, only darker.

When I looked up, the black man had gone.
90   Only my own face startled me in the dark train window.

Jackie Kay

Questions

1. The writer doesn't appear to be upset by the sudden presence of the man staring at her. How does she feel? (2)

2. 'He looked into the dark pool of my eyes' (line 5)
   'He stared into the dark depth of me' (line 15)
   What effect is gained by the repetition of the word 'dark' in these lines? (1)

3. How is the stranger's certainty about the poet's origins emphasised? (2)

4. Consider the reference to the train's journey (lines 22–24). How might we consider the train's journey to be a metaphor for what the poet is experiencing? (2)

5. 'People were walking down the trembling aisle' (line 31)
   How effective is this line in conveying the atmosphere of the situation? (2)

6. In what sense is the poet's face a 'map' (line 35)? (2)

7. What is implied about the poet's relationship with her father (line 40)? (1)

8. As the journey progresses how does the poet view the stranger? (2)

9. 'a MacLachlan, a MacDonnell, a MacLeod' (line 52)
   How effective are these references in making the poet's point? (2)

10. What does the poet's repetition of her request, 'Tell me about the Ibos' (lines 50 and 58), tell us about her mood? (1)

11. How are we made aware of the poet's pride in her new sense of identity (lines 66–67)? (1)

12. 'If the grandparents are alive' (line 75)
    What does this qualification make us realise about the vision being portrayed by the stranger? (2)

13. Consider how the image of dance is used in the penultimate verse (lines 80–86). (3)

14. Why might the poet's own face startle her (line 90)? (2)

15. Consider the title of the poem. In what ways is the poem about pride? (2)

16. How effective has the poet been in conveying to the reader the impact of this experience on her own sense of identity? (3)

[30 marks]

© Museum of Orkney

Edwin Muir was born on the island of Orkney in 1887. At the age of 14 he moved to the industrial city of Glasgow where, within four years, four members of his family, including both his parents, died. His poetry is often concerned with the idea of humanity falling from a state of natural grace because of our relentless search for apparent progress. He died in 1959. For more information about Muir visit SLAINTE (Scottish Libraries Across the Internet):
www.slainte.org.uk/Scotauth/ muiredsw.htm

or

www.rhizomatics.demon.co.uk/ muir/index.html

Textual Analysis Practice Paper G

<---- Note

The Horses

Barely a twelvemonth after
The seven days war that put the world to sleep,
Late in the evening the strange horses came.
By then we had made our covenant with silence,
5   But in the first few days it was so still
We listened to our breathing and were afraid.
On the second day
The radios failed; we turned the knobs; no answer.
On the third day a warship passed us, heading north,
10   Dead bodies piled on the deck. On the sixth day
A plane plunged over us into the sea. Thereafter
Nothing. The radios dumb;
And still they stand in corners of our kitchens,
And stand, perhaps, turned on, in a million rooms
15   All over the world. But now if they should speak,
If on a sudden they should speak again,
If on the stroke of noon a voice should speak,
We would not listen, we would not let it bring
That old bad world that swallowed its children quick
20   At one great gulp. We would not have it again.
Sometimes we think of the nations lying asleep,
Curled blindly in impenetrable sorrow,
And then the thought confounds us with its strangeness.
The tractors lie about our fields; at evening
25   They look like dank sea-monsters couched and waiting.
We leave them where they are and let them rust:
'They'll moulder away and be like other loam.'
We make our oxen drag our rusty ploughs,
Long laid aside. We have gone back
30   Far past our fathers' land.

                       And then, that evening
Late in the summer the strange horses came.
We heard a distant tapping on the road,
A deepening drumming; it stopped, went on again
35   And at the corner changed to hollow thunder.
We saw the heads
Like a wild wave charging and were afraid.
We had sold our horses in our fathers' time
To buy new tractors. Now they were strange to us
40   As fabulous steeds set on an ancient shield
Or illustrations in a book of knights.
We did not dare go near them. Yet they waited,
Stubborn and shy, as if they had been sent
By an old command to find our whereabouts
45   And that long-lost archaic companionship.
In the first moment we had never a thought
That they were creatures to be owned and used.

Among them were some half-a-dozen colts
Dropped in some wilderness of the broken world,
50   Yet new as if they had come from their own Eden.
Since then they have pulled our ploughs and borne our loads,
But that free servitude still can pierce our hearts.
Our life is changed; their coming our beginning

Edwin Muir

Questions

1. What event is described at the start of the poem?   (1)

2. Can you suggest a reason why the silence surrounding the survivors might make them 'afraid' (line 6)?   (1)

3. How does the poet convey the breakdown of technology?   (2)

4. 'Dead bodies piled on the deck.' (line 10)
   How effective do you find the image created here?   (2)

5. Consider the writer's use of repetition in lines 15–18. How does this help convey the feelings of the survivors?   (2)

6. 'That old bad world that swallowed its children quick
   At one great gulp.' (lines 19–20)
   Comment on the effectiveness of the image being used here.   (2)

7. How effective is the writer's use of simile to describe the tractors? (line 25)   (2)

8. 'We have gone back
   Far past our fathers' land.' (lines 29–30)
   What is being suggested in these lines about the lifestyle of the survivors?   (2)

9. Consider the references to sound made in lines 33–35. How does the poet use these to shatter the sense of silence created in the first verse?   (4)

10. 'We saw the heads
    Like a wild wave charging and were afraid.' (lines 36–37)
    Comment on the contrasting sources of the survivors' fear in verse 1 and verse 2.   (2)

11. a) In what way might the horses be regarded as being 'strange' (line 39)?   (1)

    b) Comment on the general description of the horses contained in lines 40–41.   (1)

12. What might the 'long-lost archaic companionship' (line 45) refer to? How was it lost?   (2)

13. Why does the poet mention the birth of the colts?   (2)

14. Look at the last line of the poem. In what way has the arrival of the horses meant a new beginning for the survivors?   (2)

15. How effective has the poet been in conveying a particular viewpoint in this poem?   (2)

[30 marks]

Textual Analysis Answer Section

Textual Analysis A - Answer Guide

1. Reference to 'widest' as suggesting space, unlimited and 'fences' suggesting enclosures, boundaries.

2. Because they have experienced the 'electric' fences and learned not to touch them.

3. a) 'Not' coming first emphasises the negative about where they are, 'here'; whilst the structure also underlines the idea of 'anywhere' being an acceptable alternative.

   b) Could have been a conclusion to previous statement 'anywhere beyond the wires' but used as a link to second stanza suggesting that the thought of beyond the wires is what motivates the cattle into their 'blunder'.

4. 'blunder' has connotations of unthinking mistake of significant proportion.

   'muscle-shredding' suggests the violence of the action as if muscle being ripped apart.

   'no quarter' - showing no mercy, like soldiers in battle.

5. a) That they give up hoping to move beyond the wires.

   b) 'widest senses' - widest echoes previous use in relation to prairies; senses suggests not just a sense of smell but the idea of a zest for life, adventure.

6. The young cattle learn from bitter experience not to touch the electric fence or they will be injured - this leads to them curbing their aspiration to seek fresher water, to see what is out there.

   The parallel would be young people who have their horizons limited by what they experience in their lives, e.g. poverty, poor education, etc. These things would act like the electric fences on the cattle - they limit the possibilities of life.

1. a) You should comment on the elaborate, ornate, expensive style of lighting suggested by chandeliers in comparison with the basic, stark image of the single bulb.

   Comment on 'stagey' might suggest falseness of chandelier opulence, compared with the harsher reality of single light.

   b) Answers should suggest idea of basic working conditions or sense of poverty.

   c) *'celebrate'; suggests pride, recognition of worth.*

2. *He uses the word 'powering', which conveys his wonderment, awe, at the force of the sewing machine.*

3. Similarity will probably refer to the literal speed of typing/sewing.

   The writer uses a typewriter to create his poems and writing. In the same way his mother uses the sewing machine to create clothes.

   Two marks for matching ideas of creativity.
   One mark for references to nimbleness of movement.

4. For two marks, you should suggest the idea of the boy being transfixed/captivated/mesmerised/hypnotised by the working of the machine.
   One mark for references to being interested in it.

5. *It creates a break between the time change of night to day, but also between the watching process and the wearing of the clothes.*

6. a) *The poet develops the image of music and sound. He refers to the machine as a 'powerful instrument', which could be both a mechanical and a musical instrument. He then talks about a 'purring' sound and finally refers to the finished clothes as his mother's 'songs', as if they were musical creations.*

   b) *Operas are grand-scale musical productions where life is conducted in song. It is as if he sees his mother's craft as being equal in grandeur to any opera.*

   Note ⤏

   Opera is in fact the Latin word for 'works', further underlining the poet's purpose in celebrating his mother's hard work.

7. You should refer to the poem in order to support your answers.

   You should generally regard the poem as being effective: for example, sense of wonderment portrayed through word choice: 'powering', 'brilliant'; sense of pride about his mother: 'celebrate'; 'wearing her songs'.

Textual Analysis C - Answer Guide

1. *Certain words help us understand the mood. 'Discontent' suggests that they are aggrieved; 'earnest' suggests that they are in a serious frame of mind; and 'full of the fire of battle' tells us that they are prepared to fight.*

   The writer also uses a sustained metaphor, the blazing fire, to carry forward the idea that the men are determined to fight for their rights.

2. a) *The repetition gives additional emphasis to the notion of passion, suggesting that it is widely felt.*

   b) *In the first instance it is developed to reflect a sense of adventure: 'full, daring'; in the second instance its uniqueness to the situation is emphasised: 'strange', 'never felt before'.*

3. *'Confident' suggests that they believe they will win the struggle but 'exuberantly' conveys an additional sense of their overflowing excitement and enthusiasm.*

4. *'aristocrat and gentleman'*

5. *Each clause begins with a participle/verb - 'abandoning', 'ignoring', 'choosing' - conveying a sense of doing things, action.*

   The three clauses build up a cumulative effect of Captain White brushing aside all objections.

6. *'toil-worn, care-lined faces' and 'heavy ordeal'.*

   Both these phrases create a more sombre tone as they suggest the hardships that the men have suffered and the difficulties they face. They are in contrast to the idea of a 'glow' in the men's faces and the sense of being 'full of the fire of battle' in paragraph 1. The one long sentence that makes up paragraph 2 adds to the sombreness.

7. Answers should suggest the effectiveness of the writer.

   Good answers will talk about the personification of the 'Artist Sun' and lively detail of the colourful sunset.

   You should then discuss how the colours are described as symbolic of the men's mood, hopes and fears.

8. Again, you should answer in a positive mode although any answer justified by textual reference is acceptable.

   The paragraph should be regarded as effective as a sense of growing anticipation, established in the first three paragraphs, is brought to a head by the opening of the window.

1. *Creates a certain clinical cold feel to the location; impersonal.*

2. 'like a damaged insect'; damaged suggesting broken or wounded in some way; insect – inconsequential.

   Metaphor – 'jumbo size dentist's drill'; jumbo suggesting oversized, elephantine; 'dentist's drill' something generally regarded as unpleasant.

   Combination suggests a vaguely critical, negative tone – wry disregard.

3. a) 'But' signals a time change from day to night and a change of mood from mild unease to something more sinister.

   b) Personification of 'midnight' as being some kind of 'foreign' invader.
      Use of the adjective 'uncivilised' to suggest the kind of behaviour to be found in the city at night.

   c) Refers to the act of residents switching on their lights. Key idea relates to 'shot at', which suggests the idea of armed conflict, as if people are defending themselves against the invader (midnight); effective link to the idea of a gun flash as it is being shot.
      'million' reminds us of the scale of the city.

      'all ups and acrosses' – a reference to the street grid that applies in New York, but also conveys the image of different lights being on in a high-rise building, making it resemble a crossword, a conundrum.

4. *The technology that he finds himself surrounded by, distractions to take his mind away from what is happening in the street.*

5. Linking the ululating noises as being warhoops from Native Americans and also the sound of sirens in the street.

   Reference to the glittering canyons and gulches referring to the geography of the 'Wild West' but also representing the high-sided streets of modern New York with its tall buildings and neon lights.

6. References: 'broken bones'
                'harsh screaming'   } accept developed comment
                'blood glazed on the sidewalk'.   on at least two

7. a) *The boundary between civilised behaviour and savagery. He is suggesting that it is how we choose to behave not where we live that marks out civilisation. The frontier is within each of us.*

   b) *Very effective. Acts as a conclusion to the ideas in the poem in relation to New York but also serves to universalise the statement so that we could apply it to any city or town.*

In textual analysis, it is possible for a number of answers to be considered correct, as a certain amount of personal interpretation of the text is acceptable. The key point is that any opinion must be clearly explained by detailed reference to the text.

Textual Analysis E - Answer Guide

←···· Note

1. *The comparison being made links the now obsolete weapons lying wasting in the desert to the skeletal teeth of ancient prehistoric dinosaurs, the brontosauri. It is effective in a number of ways: for example, 'monument' could suggest a memorial of some sort, echoing tributes to the dead of many wars; more directly it suggests that in this future world weapons of destruction are as extinct as the dinosaurs are today.*

2. *To suggest that 'They' are an omnipotent power, like God.*

3. *'The computers had found a formula for plenty' suggests that technological science has been applied to the production of food to feed the planet. It implies that the food is not a natural product but one designed to meet a purpose; 'formula' with its mathematical connotations suggests this.*

   'Immortality came wrapped in polythene' refers to the idea in the poem that all human parts can be replaced by artificially produced substitutes to the point where humans can live forever. 'Polythene' connects the image to wrapping used by shops to package goods, and also reflects the man-made nature of the whole process.

4. a) *'machine-tooled brains'. The poet's choice of language here suggests that people's brains, and subsequently their capacity to think, are being shaped and sized in the way that a piece of metal or wood might be treated in a workshop or factory. It hints at people being shaped and controlled, as if they were being mass-produced in a factory rather than being free-thinking individuals.*

   'Each idea was sterilized before its issue.
   The computers fixed a safety-mark for thinking.'

   This continues the idea that free thinking is not permitted as ideas are cleansed/purified to ensure that everyone thinks and feels the same. 'Sterilized' is effective as it links with the idea of sterility, lifelessness. The computers control everything, even what people are allowed to think.

   b) *What concerns the poet most is that the capacity for free thought and action is being removed.*

5. *The word 'changeless' suggests a monotonous, repetitive existence, emphasised by the use of the word 'endless'. The tone of the line is ironic as the 'happiness' referred to is lifeless and soulless.*

6. *A single individual, deliberately understated as being 'small' and who may be seen as naturally rebellious as a result of his red hair, escapes to the hills to live a different kind of life. His actions inspire others who are similarly discontented with the manufactured illusion of perfection in the world in which they are living. Unable to comprehend or cope with this exercise in free will, the computers and the system they support break down.*

7. *'fury' or 'rage'*

8. *It suggests the dawn of a new era.*

9. *The computers have been responsible for the dulling of any emotional feeling other than supposed happiness. Personification is used to portray them as 'crying', one of the feelings they are supposed to have eradicated.*

10. *The parallel is with the Biblical story of creation where God creates the world in six days and then rests on the seventh. The structure of the poem suggests a similar re-creation of the world by 'They'. It is appropriate as it suggests the idea of society using science to 'play God', attempting to create a 'perfect' world.*

11. You would be expected to state McIlvanney's main theme, and then to evaluate his success by detailed reference to the text. It is acceptable to expand upon points you may already have covered in earlier answers.

    McIlvanney is clearly warning about the dangers posed by genetic engineering and suggesting to us that our weaknesses and faults are part of what makes us human in the first place.

    Reference should then be made to a number of points, including:
    - Use of similes – 'like molar monuments...'
    - Effective imagery within the poem, e.g. the clinical removal of feelings, 'Mind-mechanics, They located every hatred, Extracted it, and amputated angers.'
    - How the writer conveys the idea of conditioned behaviour – 'But as long as there was light the people smiled.'
    - The structure of the poem.
    - The title, which combines the words Eugenics and Genesis to create a new portmanteau word that clearly depicts the theme of the poem.

    Note ⋯⟩

    - The sense of hope portrayed in the final stanza.

Portmanteau – a term first used by Lewis Carroll to describe a word that has been created by joining together two existing words. For example, eugenics and genesis to create *Eugenesis*; or lithe and slimy to give slithy.

Textual Analysis F - Answer Guide

1. Possibilities for answers might include: intrigued, comfortable, in awe, connected in an inexplicable way. Reference should be made to the idea that a bond was established, 'as if he and I went a long way back'; and an experience being shared, 'like something being given from one to the other'.

2. It suggests the idea of something hidden away, out of sight; something until now unknown, mysterious or untapped about the poet's past.

3. The repetition three times of 'Ibo', along with 'definitely' and his emphatic 'thumping' of the table.

4. The train's journey is a metaphor for the poet's journey into her past, the 'unwritten stops in the blackness' being the history she doesn't know.

5. It is effective as it suggests the movement of the train and anyone trying to walk in it. 'Trembling' in particular conveys the emotional intensity and a sense of anticipation, but also the sense of a slight fear at the vehemence (or forcefulness) of the stranger.

6. The stranger is drawn to her at first by her facial features, which he identifies as being Ibo. He continues to explore her identity, reacting to her expressions. The map is of her life and ancestry.

7. The fact that she has 'heard' her father's name, rather than has been told it by him, suggests that she is estranged in some way from him, or may never have met or known him at all.

8. She sees him as a confidant and at different points in his explanations of life in Nigeria she imagines him to be like absent members of her family.

9. The poet feels a sense of pride at belonging to the Ibo tribe, in the same way that some people take pride in belonging to a Scottish clan, the names of three of them being listed to make the point effectively. It is an effective comparison between the clans in Scotland and African tribes, as both have a similar sense of pride and common identity.

10. That she is eager to learn more.

11. She describes both her smile and her teeth as being Ibo.

12. It makes us realise that, in a sense, the scenario is a hypothetical one as no actual family connection is established.

13. Dance is used firstly to indicate the welcome the poet imagines as the old people dance towards her. It then represents her own happiness as she begins to dance with them. But she is dancing a dance she never knew before. It's as if her spirit has found its home, and she is enlivened by her new sense of identity.

14. She is perhaps surprised as she expected to see the stranger's face, but more importantly she is seeing her own face differently because of the experience. It is as if she is looking at a stranger or a new person in the sudden reality around her.

15. Pride refers to the obvious pride the stranger has in his own identity as an Ibo, whom he regards as honourable people, and it refers to the writer's pride in making the connection to a sense of her own roots and history.

16. There are many acceptable ways of achieving full marks here. The key is to make detailed reference to the text in order to support your ideas, which in this example would be made up of identifying:
   - the family connection the poet feels she makes with the man
   - the sense of journey to establish a greater awareness of herself and her roots
   - her physical identification with the Ibos
   - her sense of new life, symbolised by her dance.

Textual Analysis G - Answer Guide

1. A nuclear/chemical/biological war.

2. They have lived for so long in a world full of noise and hustle and bustle that they are unused to the quietness.

3. Primarily through the image of the radios failing, which represents a breakdown in communication. The image of the plane plunging out of control also suggests technology has failed.

4. This rather gruesome image is very effective and conveys graphically the scale of the casualties, heaped in undignified mounds as if for waste disposal.

5. Repetition of the words 'if' and 'speak' is used to convey a sense of fear and panic; the idea of sound breaking their vale of silence frightening the survivors. The repetition of 'we' is also used to emphasise their determination not to return to the way things were; 'We would not ...'.

6. The writer uses personification very effectively here to convey how the world destroyed itself like a cannibalistic mother eating her children. 'Swallowed' and 'one great gulp' are particularly effective as they capture the idea of nuclear explosions consuming the Earth in a short period of time.

7. *It is effective as the idea of sea monsters suggests people's fears are based on their imagination, in the way that sailors once feared creatures they had never seen. 'Couched and waiting' also suggests a beast of prey, ready to spring out and attack them.*

8. *That they have reverted to a more simple and basic lifestyle, rejecting the world they inherited and the technology that accompanied it for the more natural world of their ancestors.*

9. *'a distant tapping' and 'a deepening drumming'. The onomatopoeic quality of these words helps break the silence of the first stanza, 'covenant with silence'. This is further developed by the reference to 'hollow thunder' and the connotation of a gathering storm.*

    Better answers will also mention the alliteration of 'deepening drumming' and may make reference to the sense of primal instinct contained within the image of drumming or suggest the idea of a heartbeat, like new life.

10. This simile is full of energy and life, a sharp contrast to the images in the first stanza of death and silence. You must remark upon the source of the first fear being the silence, whilst the source of the second is the noise and its accompanying vitality.

11. a) *Strange, as in unknown to them.*

    b) *The horses are described as being at their most majestic, 'fabulous steeds set on an ancient shield'; they represent a positive image in contrast to the negative ones of the first verse.*

12. *Humanity's bond/relationship with nature. Lost through an over dependence on technology and attempts to subjugate nature to human aims.*

13. *They are symbolic of new life in the 'wilderness' of the destroyed world; a suggestion of hope.*

14. *The survivors are able to make progress again but this time with a clearer understanding of the need to control technological progress rather than become slaves to it.*

15. This answer is to some extent subjective, but whatever your view you must support it with reference to the text. For example:

    The writer has been very effective. In stanza one he clearly depicts the dangers of technology becoming an end in itself by showing the destruction that might be caused through nuclear war, the nuclear bomb being an ultimate symbol of technology. However, in stanza two he suggests that if we learn to live in harmony with nature, represented by the horses, there may still be hope for us.

Literature

Critical Essay

Introduction

You are required to write two critical essays in the formal external assessment. For your personal studies folio you also have to write a critical essay on a text of your own choosing, as an internal unit assessment.

The skills required for both assessments are essentially the same. They build upon the work you did at Standard Grade for your reading folio, where most candidates submit three critical essays.

Purpose of the Assessment

Essentially, a critical essay is designed to test your ability to respond thoughtfully to a literary text, be it a poem, a play, a novel or a short story. The marker wishes to know if you have understood the writer's purpose, if you appreciate the writer's craft, and if you can demonstrate a genuine personal response to the text.

Many students are tempted to 'learn' so-called model answers but these cannot possibly respond effectively to an unseen question. The need to respond to the actual assignment detailed is of paramount importance; that is the test!

Nature of the Assessment

In order to display your ability to write critically you will be required to produce an essay in response to a set task. Specifically, you are required to demonstrate competence in the following areas:

1. #### Understanding
   This refers to your ability to demonstrate, as appropriate to the task set, your understanding of the key aspects and main issues of the text(s) studied. This will require you to identify significant details in the text(s). In other words, are you able to respond to the central theme of the text(s) and not simply recount the detail of the narrative?

2. #### Analysis
   You are expected to explain ways in which aspects of structure, style and language contribute to the meaning and effect of the text. This involves selecting relevant quotations or referring to appropriate incidents/detail in the text in order to support the points you are making.

3. #### Evaluation
   This is where you show that you have thought about what the writer is saying and how he/she is saying it, and have in some way engaged with the ideas in the text. Part of the evaluation process is linked to analysis and requires you to comment on how effective the writer has been in the quotations or detail you have referred to. Evaluation also includes, as relevant to the chosen question, your genuine response to the ideas expressed by the writer in the text you are discussing.

4. #### Expression
   This is about how you organise your answer to respond clearly to the task by presenting a clear line of thought in your argument. It also refers to your use of appropriate critical terminology, e.g. reference to characterisation; setting; the use of rhyme (see Appendix A, page 106). Expressing yourself well in an essay requires good writing skills: word choice, sentencing, punctuation and paragraphing are all important.

These four performance criteria should not be seen as distinct, separate requirements as a good critical essay creates a holistic impression on the marker as a result of these different areas interacting. However, each element is required to be present in order for you to pass the assessment.

How to Tackle

The texts you read will be of a good quality. The teacher will have chosen them because he/she thinks that they have something to tell the reader about life; about human beings and the world we live in. This is what marks out the key difference between literature and pulp fiction: literature has something to say to the reader about the human condition; it is not merely there to entertain the reader, although it most often does that as well.

Your task is to reveal to the marker your understanding of the writer's message/thematic concern, and your reaction to it.

How Do You Do This?

Firstly, it will never be enough to simply retell the narrative (storyline) of a text. Nor is a straightforward 'review' type answer sufficient – you must respond to the question set. In the exam, one of the main reasons for students failing this section is because of an inadequate response to the instructions in the question (i.e. there is no clear line of thought based on the task set).

Your approach to the task must be focused on the assignment. It is your ability to respond to the task (the question) that allows you to demonstrate your understanding of the key elements, central concerns and significant details of the text(s).

Answers that have clearly been prepared before the exam and then twisted in some way to fit the question being asked will invariably achieve a poor mark because of lack of relevance to the task. 'Topping and tailing' (sticking in a reference to the task in the first and last paragraph and then filling the rest of the essay with a stock response) is a common feature of essays that fail to achieve a pass mark. If you wish to pass, do not adopt this approach.

It is absolutely essential, therefore, in the external examination that you respond directly to the question.

A simple but effective way of achieving this focus is to create a title for your essay based on the detail of the task. This will set up the type of specific response required. Remember this is a working title for your benefit. It is not part of your answer and it does not have to be catchy or clever. The simplest way to create a good title is to take the words of the question and refocus them.

Once you have done this, write the title down, draw a balloon around it and then brainstorm some ideas for your essay. This is an effective method of planning your essay, particularly in the exam where time is limited.

Example, using Ray Bradbury's novel *Fahrenheit 451*

Note ⸱⸱⸱⸱>

Task:

Consider a novel that has something important to say about the world in which we live. By examining the use of character, setting and plot show how the writer has successfully conveyed his/her message to the reader.

An appropriate title and plan here might be:

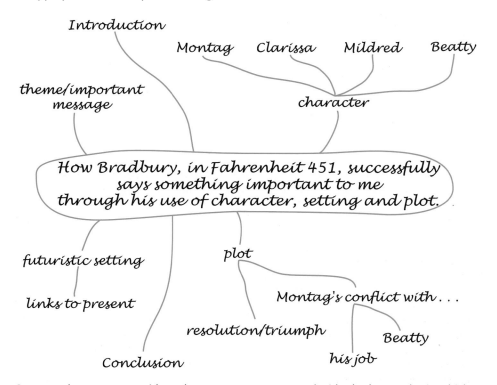

Once you have got some ideas down on paper, you can decide the best order in which to deal with them (perhaps number them on your plan). Combined with your opening paragraph and your conclusion – both of which are essential – you are now ready to tackle the actual essay writing.

Remember, the title is not actually part of your essay, so in your opening paragraph you need to home in on the task. Again, the simplest way to do this is to take the words of the question and reshape them into an opening statement. A useful mnemonic for your opening paragraph is **TART**: **T** for the title of the text; **A** for the author's name; and **RT** for reference to task.

Example:

A novel that has something important to say about the world in which we live is 'Fahrenheit 451' by Ray Bradbury. By examining his use of character, setting and plot, I will show how Bradbury has successfully conveyed his message to the reader; that message being that we need to safeguard our self-identity in an increasingly technological world that restricts individualism.

Ray Bradbury was born in 1920 and he became one of America's best writers, being particularly well known for his science fiction work. Several of his books and short stories have been made into movies and he has written numerous film and television scripts. One of his short stories, *The Pedestrian*, contained some of the thematic ideas developed more fully in *Fahrenheit 451* and it is well worth reading. If you wish to study *Fahrenheit 451*, a useful site to view is www.sparknotes.com/lit/451/ You should also look at Ray Bradbury's homepage: www.RayBradbury.com

Using the language of the task to create your opening paragraph sets up a clear approach to a successful essay.

From here you should continue to develop your response. Pay particular attention to the structure of your paragraphs. You should open with a statement relevant to the question; follow with evidence from the text; explain the connection; and then finish with a comment. This pattern will enable you to establish a successful line of thought and to meet the other performance criteria.

S	Statement
E	Evidence
E	Explanation
C	Comment

Example:

Statement

Bradbury uses the character of Mildred, Montag's wife, to highlight the emptiness and futility of life in the novel's futuristic setting.

Evidence

When we first meet Mildred, she is having her stomach pumped as she has just attempted suicide. The description of this operation conveys a cold and mechanistic approach to life: 'They had this machine … the impersonal operator. Not unlike the digging of a trench …'

Explanation

By describing this scene with such matter-of-fact language, Bradbury successfully reveals how little life is valued in this future world. It's as if Mildred was worth no more than a disused car that is being serviced.

Comment

Her world is an empty hollow with no sense of purpose. It is made clear in the rest of the novel that far from being abnormal, Mildred in fact represents the norm of life in the future – a norm that Montag rebels against.

This would form quite a compact paragraph, demonstrating each of the skills required by the marker – Understanding, Analysis, Evaluation and Expression.

Bradbury uses the character of Mildred, Montag's [Understanding] *wife, to highlight the emptiness and futility of life in the novel's futuristic setting. When we first meet Mildred, she is having her stomach pumped as she has just attempted suicide. The description of* [Analysis] *this operation conveys a cold and mechanistic approach to life: 'They had this machine … the impersonal operator. Not unlike the digging of a trench …' By describing this scene with such matter-of-fact language, Bradbury successfully reveals how little life is valued in this* [Evaluation] *future world. It's as if Mildred was worth no more than a* [Understanding] *disused car that is being serviced. Her world is an empty hollow with no sense of purpose. It is made* [Expression] *clear in the rest of the novel that far from being abnormal, Mildred in fact represents the norm of life in the future – a norm that Montag rebels against.*

Note ┄┄⟩

Of critical importance is the linking together of your argument (Expression). This will be done primarily through the statements and will create your line of thought. In a good critical essay, the marker should be able to read the topic sentences of each paragraph and see in them a clear and logical sequence of argument. A good test for your own work is to highlight your statements and then read them together as if they were a single paragraph. If there isn't a natural flow, your line of thought is weak.

Note ┄┄⟩

For your personal study and for class essays you may wish to make a more detailed plan, utilising SEEC to create an outline for your essay.

Consider the exemplar below, which uses *Hotel Room, 12th floor* as its text.

Task – to consider the poem's relevance to the modern world and to examine MacCaig's use of setting, imagery, word-choice and structure.

Introduction:		A poem that is relevant to the modern world is *Hotel Room, 12th floor* by Norman MacCaig. In this poem, MacCaig explores the idea that beneath the trappings of civilisation we are still basically savage human beings. To do this he makes effective use of setting, imagery, word-choice and structure.
Para	Statement:	MacCaig sets the poem in New York City but he seems distinctly unimpressed by the sights offered by one of the world's great cities.
	Evidence:	simile and metaphor used
	Explanation:	negative, inconsequential
	Comment:	NYC seen as impressive by most but MacCaig unmoved.
Para	Statement:	If MacCaig is dismissive towards New York by day, he makes effective use of imagery to suggest something more sinister as night approaches.
	Evidence:	personification of midnight, image of 'shot at'
	Explanation:	like an attacker that needs to be repelled
	Comment:	MacCaig disturbed by sense of violence.

This pattern can be repeated until you have covered all the areas under consideration.

Conclusion:	MacCaig's poem makes a bold and effective statement that suggests to the reader that whilst modern society may have made great technological progress, the real measure of our advance as human beings still remains how we behave and treat one another.

SEEC is not a four-sentence formula. It will often take two or three sentences to make an effective statement and the evidence and evaluation parts will certainly be more extended. SEEC is a general shape for each paragraph.

Another 'mnemonic' you might find useful, and which is printed on all your exam papers, is SQA(!) – Statement, Quotation, Analysis.

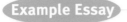

Example Essay

The following essay is based on the poem *Eugenesis*, which you studied as a textual analysis task earlier in the book. In this essay, the knowledge gained from analysing the poem is used to write effectively about it, in response to the kind of assignment you will find in the critical essay section of the examination.

Assignment

Choose a poem that deals with an important topic. Consider carefully the poet's use of various techniques such as word choice, structure and imagery. How effective has he/she been in conveying a particular viewpoint?

How McIlvanney successfully conveys his viewpoint on an important topic in the poem 'Eugenesis'.

A poem that deals effectively with an important topic is 'Eugenesis' by William McIlvanney. This is a sardonic portrayal of a future society in which computerised technology has created a perfect world order. McIlvanney's poem echoes today's society where human cloning is openly talked about, the genetic modification of food is already happening and the internet is an increasingly used resource.

McIlvanney creates a portmanteau word, combining the words Eugenics and Genesis, to present a clever and intriguing title that encapsulates the key theme of the poem. 'Eugenesis' is a poem which looks at how people, given supreme creative ability through scientific knowledge, are most likely to use this knowledge for unintended, destructive, perhaps even evil ends, rather than to promote goodness and the welfare of others. Eugenics is the science of racial 'purification' by means of genetic engineering. This was most prominently practised by the Nazis during World War II. By part using the word 'Genesis', found in the Jewish Torah and the Christian Bible, within the title of the poem, McIlvanney is contrasting an ancient account of divine creation against that which some people of the future may pursue so that they can be 'gods' and control life.

McIlvanney continues this parallel with the creation of the world in the actual structure of the poem. The first seven stanzas each represent a day in the creation of the new world, and each deals with a new aspect of the perfected society except the last which details a rebellion, the consequence of which is developed in the eighth stanza. I found this structure straightforward and easy to follow and the reference to the story of creation was clear.

McIlvanney begins the poem with examples of positive developments that the reader would welcome. War is 'eradicated' and the 'starving' are fed. He makes use of a complicated but clever simile in describing the discarded bombs as being 'like molar monuments to brontosauri sentenced to extinction'. This captures the idea of war being a thing of the past, as the dinosaurs are part of our past. It took me a moment to follow through the poet's imagery here and this helped reinforce the poet's vision of the enormity of humanity's achievement in ending conflict.

McIlvanney, however, has already introduced hints that this perfect world has unpleasant aspects to it. In the second stanza, the word 'They' is given a capital letter suggesting an omnipotent force of some sort being in charge, rather than the people themselves. This is underlined by reference to the computers finding a 'formula for plenty'. In this regard, the fact that the 'smiles were uniform' hints at people being controlled and conditioned in an unacceptable way, despite the material gains provided. The ambiguity of this phrase was not apparent at first, but on a re-reading of the poem its more sinister implications became obvious.

This idea of conditioned behaviour and external control is carried forward by words such as 'processed' and 'machine-tooled' whose connotations suggest an assembly line approach to living. The computers - which 'thought of everything' - appear to be in complete control.

McIlvanney even foresees a situation where death itself is made redundant: 'death was dead'. His use of alliteration here emphasises the abruptness of this process. In this Frankenstein world of the future every human part becomes available off the shelf: 'immortality came wrapped in polythene', that is, any body part can be replaced. This, in fact, is one of the main arguments used today to support the cloning of human genes so perhaps McIlvanney's view of the future is not so fantastical.

But it is not only physical repair that is possible. This futuristic world also envisages a form of mind control: negative feelings such as hatred are removed by 'mind-mechanics'. More dangerously, ideas and free-thinking are limited by a 'safety mark' created by the computers. In this perfect world, people are not to be allowed freedom of thought, as this might result in something the computers cannot control.

Life became meaningless. It appears to be perfect – 'endless happiness' – but it is empty of all the emotions and feelings and thoughts that make human beings different from other animals.

Finally someone rebels – 'a small man with red hair'. He steals a tent and heads for the hills. He writes one word, possibly 'fury' or 'rage', and leaves it behind for the computers, which translate it as 'irrational anger'. Contrary to the world of the computers this man feels emotions.

McIlvanney uses the image of a 'contagious' disease to suggest how this feeling rapidly spread to the rest of the population, 'ran like a rash'. This is effective, as in the sanitised future of these computers, all such 'illnesses' have been wiped out and it is as if the 'machines' have no defences: natural order is restored, 'the sunset was unauthorized' and its beauty causes the dawn chorus of the 'metal cocks' to crow, symbolising the dawn of a new, more natural order.

McIlvanney employs ironic personification to end the poem when the computers, in trying to understand the sound of laughter, seize up and begin to 'cry'.

The message of McIlvanney's poem is clear: he sees as intrinsic to what makes us human all the frailties and faults that 'They' would wish to wipe out. He appears to be of the view that it is our very vulnerability that makes us who and what we are. A futuristic world where all evils are removed is one to be welcomed but not, he argues, if it comes at the price of reducing human life to a mere existence, devoid of all feeling and emotion, conditioned and programmed to remove all individuality.

As suggested at the beginning of this essay, the technology to create such a future is now with us – 'Eugenesis' is a timely warning of some of the dangers presented by these new technologies.

The *coloured type* highlights key statements that create the **line of thought**. If you read over only the coloured type, you should have a sense of coherence – as if there is a logical flow to the ideas being presented. Your own essays should have a similarly structured line of thought.

←···· Note

Thematic links

Schools will often study texts around a particular theme. Here, for example, we have looked at *Fahrenheit 451*, *Eugenesis* and we have also tried a close reading passage about 'Andi'. These are all clearly linked to concerns about the kind of world we may inhabit in the not so distant future. Studying texts in a thematic way allows you to build up a broader knowledge and understanding of the topic and should help you to respond more effectively in assessments.

If you are interested in this particular thematic content you might wish to read George Orwell's *Nineteen Eighty-Four* and Aldous Huxley's *Brave New World*, both of which are modern classics exploring the idea of dystopian society. The opposite of dystopia is utopia, which comes from the title of a book by Sir Thomas More of the same name. In More's book, utopia is an imaginary perfect society against which real human societies are compared and satirised. *Utopia* is available to read online at the following webpage:
www.constitution.org/tm/utopia.htm

Listed below are National Qualification-style assignments for critical essay writing. You should plan out answers for the texts you are studying and try writing some of the essays. Before each section of the paper there will be a box containing useful advice about dealing with the central concern(s) of the text(s) and an indication of the techniques appropriate to the genre being tackled e.g. structure, climax and plot in relation to prose; key scene and dialogue for drama; imagery, word choice and mood for poetry. These are useful reminders about some of the techniques that you should be referring to in your essay.

Choose a play where setting is of key importance to the text.
Discuss how the setting contributes to the characterisation within the play and to the main thematic concern(s) of the writer.

Choose a play where the conflict between two characters climaxes in a specific scene or incident.
Explain the nature of the conflict and show how the scene in question leads you to a greater understanding of the play as a whole.

Choose a novel or short story where the main character struggles against the society in which he/she lives.
Briefly explain the reasons behind his/her dilemma and indicate how the resolution of the conflict highlights the play's main theme.

Choose a novel where the conclusion has a definite tone of either optimism or pessimism.
Explain why you consider it to be a fitting ending and show in detail how it links to the rest of the text.

Choose a poem which deals with an intensely personal experience but still has something universal to say.
Show how the poet has managed to achieve both of these aspects.

Choose a poem where the poet has explored an aspect of nature in a way that appeals to you.
State what the appeal is and then in some detail consider how the poet's use of literary technique has managed to engage you interest.

Example Critical Essay

Printed below is a student's attempt at writing a critical essay using the poem *The Horses* which you read earlier as a textual analysis exercise (see page 72–73). Read it through and consider how well the student has put into practice some of the suggestions you have been studying.

Assignment

Choose a poem that made you think more deeply about an aspect of life. Consider carefully the poet's use of various literary techniques to enhance the message of the poem.

A poem that made me think more deeply about an aspect of life is 'The Horses' by Edwin Muir. The poem is concerned with humanity's relationship with nature and in it the poet tries to suggest that we have become over-dependent on technology and have forgotten our true place in the natural order of things. The techniques used by the poet deepened my understanding of this theme and helped me realise its relevance to the world we live in.

The structure of the poem, with its two mirror-image stanzas, clearly supports Muir's exploration of this theme through an examination of technology's destructive power followed by the hope of renewal through a partnership with Earth's natural forces. The first stanza deals with the sense of destruction and despair created by the near annihilation of the world through a nuclear holocaust. Muir's word choice emphasises the dismay and fear of the small group of survivors: 'silence', 'still', 'afraid', 'nothing'. In the second stanza, however, a new resurgence of life occurs with the arrival of a herd of wild horses: 'drumming', 'charging', 'like a wild wave'. The horses, symbolic of nature, bring fresh hope to the survivors and ultimately produce an optimistic note to the poem. Close examination of the two stanzas shows them to be mirror images of each other: the first dominated by pessimism – the second by a sense of hope. This hope is conditioned by the need to understand the earlier mistake that had been made in mankind becoming over-reliant on technology. The warning given by the poet seems to me to be increasingly relevant today.

By adopting the persona of a survivor, Muir humanises the poem's message and skilfully avoids making the poem too didactic in tone.

Muir's use of imagery is very effective. The survivors have become scared of the 'old bad world' that has destroyed itself and the image of a cannibalistic mother is deployed to convey fear and horror: 'that swallowed its children quick At one great gulp'. This is particularly effective as it conveys the sense of a nuclear explosion sucking up the Earth in its power but also because its gruesome connotations emphasise the reason for a complete rejection of the old world and its values by the few survivors.

Technology is now seen as a threat to the survivors' new-found tranquillity, their 'covenant with silence'. Muir uses an effective simile to convey their fear when he describes the now discarded tractors as being 'like dank sea-monsters couched and waiting'. Despite their unease, however, the survivors have rejected technology and modelled their lives on early human communities with simple farming: 'We make our oxen drag our rusty ploughs … We have gone back Far past our fathers' land'.

If the poem had finished at this point it would still make sense – humanity had destroyed its world through the ultimate symbol of the technology it had become too reliant on – the atomic bomb. As a consequence, it had reverted to an almost primitive way of life in order to survive. But Muir wants us to think further about the issue he is exploring. He wants us to consider not only what is being lost by humanity's alienation from the natural world but also what is to be gained by reconnecting with it. It was this aspect of the poem that most directly made me think about the modern world where we seem to be indifferent to the damage we are doing to the planet.

In the second stanza, Muir builds upon some of the Biblical references made in stanza one ('seven days war'; 'covenant'). The horses that have arrived to bring fresh hope to the survivors are described as having been sent 'By an old command' to rebuild 'that long-lost archaic companionship'. Whilst some might take this as being a reference to the idea of a creator re-establishing order in the world, to me it is simply a reference to the concept of balance, a natural order, where human beings are partners with nature, not abusers of it.

Muir continues the established imagery to further suggest the idea of a natural equilibrium when he describes that amongst the herd are some newborn colts, symbolic of new life, fresh 'from their own Eden'. It's as if humanity is being given a second chance to re-establish a bond with nature based on a clearer understanding of our place in the grand scheme.

Indeed that is what happens as the horses are used by the community to develop: 'Our life is changed; their coming our beginning'. Their role, however, is described as 'free servitude' and with this oxymoron Muir cleverly encapsulates the idea that it is a partnership that is being established, not a domination.

Note ·····>

Oxymoron: an expression written in opposite terms, which continues to convey a contradictory truth such as 'cruel to be kind', 'a darkness visible' and 'deafening silence' (see Appendix A, page 106).

The poem made me think deeply about our role on the planet. The idea that we might destroy ourselves through our obsession with technology and the creation of ever more powerful weapons is one I am familiar with. I think the poem's real strength is in the second stanza where it becomes clear that by not living in harmony with the rest of the natural world we are, in fact, losing out to so many potential gains. Muir's poem is a homage to the restorative power of Nature and, in a world where we savage our environment on a daily basis, it provided me with an opportunity to think more deeply about this particular aspect of life.

Group Discussion

Discussion is not part of the formal assessment of your course and you may be surprised to see it featured in this book.

It is recognised by the SQA, however, that group discussion is an essential feature of a Higher English course as it is one of the most frequently used methods of exploring texts and topics in the classroom.

The following points are included to help you gain as much as you possibly can from these activities, particularly in relation to developing your own thinking on a topic.

It is important that you interact with the other candidates in your group. This involves attempting to shape the flow of the discussion and actively promote good group relations. If someone is not taking part, for example, he/she should be encouraged to participate by being asked for his/her view. This is especially important if there are strong speakers in the group who are over keen to express their own point of view. Knowing when to allow others to speak is an important skill in any group discussion.

It is likely that your group discussions will relate to one of the texts you are studying as part of the course. To get the most out of this situation, prepare thoroughly by reading over notes and thinking about what the text has to say. Having something prepared boosts your confidence.

Do not be a spectator. However interesting you find the comments made by your classmates, if you do not contribute to the discussion you will get very little from it.

When you are making a contribution it is useful to think about how good paragraphs are written. You would start with a topic sentence and then go on to develop the topic by one of a variety of methods: giving an example; using statistics or evidence; making a contrast or drawing a comparison. An oral contribution should follow a similar pattern. It is not enough simply to express an opinion without attempting to back up your viewpoint in some manner.

Here are some useful phrases to support interaction within your group:

'I agree with that point and furthermore I think...'
'I'm sorry but I don't agree with what you are saying because...'
'Can you explain that a bit more?'
'So far we are all in agreement but what about...'
'I don't agree with this but what if someone argued...'
'Let's look at this from the opposite point of view...'
'Keri, what do you think about Bryan's view?'

Remember, as well, that your body language is part of the interaction in a group – look at the person who is talking and when you are speaking, make eye contact with the other members of the group. You can rest assured that the desk has heard it all before so you do not need to look at it throughout the assignment.

Learning is an active process and group discussion an excellent approach to stimulating thought and analysis. That's why teachers use it so much in class. But you need to participate to gain – so don't sit back, speak up!

Organising Notes For Revision

For each literary text you study, you will build up a set of notes. These will be based on classwork, group discussions, teacher comment and your own work.

To make full use of your notes for study and revision, it is important that they do not remain 'static' but instead provide the basis for active thinking about the text.

When students simply read and re-read notes over and over they begin to 'learn' them parrot-fashion and this actually weakens their own ability to think creatively and lucidly about the text. This results in tired critical essays that may demonstrate sufficient knowledge about a text but are usually lacking in relevant understanding and analysis. As a result, they are weaker in responding to the actual task, as notes are simply being regurgitated without thought.

To avoid this trap, actively reorganise and expand your basic notes as you revise.
As indicated above, you will not be starting revision from scratch, as notes will have been gathered from various sources.

The following generic questions can be used as a worksheet to help you tackle most texts:

Drama and Prose

Setting   Where and when is the story set? In what way is this significant?

Storyline   What are the main stages in the development of the actual plot? In particular, which incident is the key turning point for the central characters?

Characters
A basic character sketch for prose and drama will answer the following questions:

Who?   Who is the character?
               (Name, background, relationships, characteristics)
What?   What does he/she do?
               (Consider also the consequences of his/her actions)
Why?   Why does he/she do this?
Change   What is the main change for the central character(s)? In what way is he/she different as a result of what has happened?

Theme   What issue is the writer trying to make us think about?
               How does the writer use setting and storyline to present this issue to us?
               What other techniques does the writer use to convey his/her theme (language, incident, imagery, symbolism, structure, etc.)?

Poetry
Some of the above questions can also be applied to poetry, particularly the issue of setting in time and place.

It is useful to know when a poem was written, as assignments will sometimes make reference to, for example, pre-twentieth century poetry, and also to know if the poem belongs to a particular genre of poetry: narrative, sonnet, free verse, etc.

What is the key theme of the poem?

What stance has the poet taken? (Personal, detached observer, dramatised persona, etc.)

How does the structure of the poem aid our understanding?

Which literary techniques does the poet use to explore his/her theme? This will certainly include the poet's choice of words and use of figurative language and imagery. (See Appendix A, page 106.)

Relationships Between Characters

In most prose and drama texts, we can also revise by examining the relationship between characters, as these provide the dynamic of any given plot.

Consider the example below, a character study that uses Shakespeare's *Othello* as the source text being studied.

For this exercise, we are revising the character of Othello. Asking *Who*, *What* and *Why* will give us a basic character outline such as this:

- strong military figure, appears honourable and brave
- outsider, black, although trusted by court
- married to Desdemona
- somewhat unsure of his worth in Desdemona's eyes
- becomes suspicious and jealous of his wife
- deceived by Iago's lies and plotting, driven by insane jealousy and love
- finally murders her before killing himself.

The question to ask when looking at relationships is: 'What is the nature of the conflict or bond between the character we are studying and the other main characters?'

In Othello's case there are three main pairings that we may wish to examine:

Othello	⟵┈┈⟶	Desdemona
Othello	⟵┈┈⟶	Iago
Othello	⟵┈┈⟶	Cassio

For each character in turn, we can chart the relationship and list evidence for our viewpoint. For example, Desdemona:

Othello and Desdemona

- appear to be strongly in love with each other
- Desdemona innocently champions Cassio
- Othello, made jealous by Iago, begins to suspect Desdemona and Cassio
- Desdemona is confused but stays true and loyal
- Othello, despite his love, plans Desdemona's death
- although Othello murders Desdemona, she still forgives him prior to her death.

Evidence

True love	court scene where Othello and Desdemona defend their love before the Duke and Brabantio, Desdemona's father.
Jealousy	suspicions aroused by Iago appearing to 'know' certain secrets; Othello drawn in by his own fears about his age and 'race'; handkerchief plot of Iago dupes Othello; Othello becomes irrational, resorts to violence and plans Desdemona's death.
Forgiveness	Desdemona's dying words and Othello's final speech.

As well as detailing parts of the play to support your view it is useful to list quotations for use in your essay:

> True love
> Act 1, Scene 3
> Desdemona:　　　　My noble father … But here's my husband,
> 　　　　　　　　　And so much duty as my mother showed
> 　　　　　　　　　To you, preferring you before her father,
> 　　　　　　　　　So much I challenge that I may profess
> 　　　　　　　　　Due to the Moor my lord.
>
> Act 2, Scene 1
> Othello:　　　　　If it were now to die,
> 　　　　　　　　　'Twere now to be most happy; for I fear
> 　　　　　　　　　My soul hath her content so absolute
> 　　　　　　　　　That not another comfort like to this
> 　　　　　　　　　Succeeds in unknown fate.
>
> Act 2, Scene 1
> Othello:　　　　　I cannot speak enough of this content;
> 　　　　　　　　　It stops me here; it is too much of joy.
>
> Act 4, Scene 3
> Desdemona:　　　　Beshrew me, if I would do such a wrong for the
> 　　　　　　　　　whole world.

This exercise would then be repeated for the other two pairings identified. Having focused on Othello, we would move on and analyse another character, say Iago, in a similar way.

Theme and Task

It is not only characters that can be studied with this approach; we could use it to consider one of the play's themes or in response to assignment topics. Conflict, for example, is an element of all drama:

Note ····⟩

The most obvious source of conflict in a narrative is between two or more characters. Conflict, however, can also be between a character and his/her circumstances and be internal, for example when a character struggles with a dilemma, often moral in nature.

Conflict in Othello

- Othello and himself
- Othello/Desdemona
- Iago/Othello
- Iago/Roderigo
- Roderigo/Cassio
- Cassio/Othello.

Each of these pairings can be further analysed by charting key incidents and detailing evidence in support of your analysis.

By actively exploring issues through this approach, you will develop not only your knowledge of the text but more particularly your understanding and appreciation of it, leaving you better prepared to write a good critical essay.

Personal Study

–   Written Response
–   Spoken Response

Personal Study

Introduction

In this unit, which is compulsory, you are required to carry out independent study of a text and then to respond critically to the ideas contained within it. The guidelines allow for a wide interpretation of text and you could in theory study fairly specialist areas such as the use of language in advertising or treat text as a reference to film or other media products.

For most students, however, 'text' is likely to refer to prose, poetry or drama and this advice works from that assumption, although it can be applied equally to the more specialist options.

Purpose
The primary purpose of the personal study assessment is to test your ability to respond thoughtfully and independently to a piece of literature. It is also a test of your ability to demonstrate your response by writing effectively.

Assessment
You will be required to write about the text using an approach agreed previously with your teacher. The assessment will be done within a single hour and will be tackled under controlled conditions.

During the assessment you may use an outline plan and prepared notes. However, you are only allowed a maximum of two sides of A4 paper in total. This is an open-book assignment so you are allowed to have the text beside you.

The same four key criteria apply as those for the critical essay:

1. Understanding
   This relates to the key elements, central concerns and significant details of the text. At Higher, your review will demonstrate a secure understanding of these aspects.

2. Analysis
   This is concerned with your ability to identify and discuss aspects of structure/style/language and how these contribute to the text's meaning/effect/impact.

3. Evaluation
   This requires that you reveal your engagement with the ideas of the text, including a commentary on how effective you think the writer has been. Here you make extensive use of evidence from the text.

4. Expression
   This is concerned primarily with your ability to present a clear line of thought in relation to your declared task. You will be expected to use critical terminology accurately and to write your essay in a clear and accurate fashion.

Some suggestions for personal study reading are contained in Appendix B (see pages 110–114). Although the choice of text is ultimately a matter for you, Higher candidates would be expected to read challenging texts that allow for a developed and thoughtful personal response.

How to Tackle

The key to a good critical essay in this unit is to have a carefully prepared approach to the text. This will allow your essay to display a clear line of thought (using the SEEC approach on page 86). Your teacher will certainly discuss this matter with you and offer advice on your suggestions. However, he/she is not allowed to provide you with a specific approach, as the assessment is about your own ability to think critically about your chosen text.

There are, however, some preliminary steps to follow before we are ready to discuss the writing stage.

- Your choice of book is crucial. Although you are not restricted to novels (non-fiction, poetry and drama are alternatives), these remain the most frequent choice as the novel offers the most straightforward approach to this task. It is important that you choose a text of quality, as it will provide you with much more material to write about. In theory, you are free to choose any text but a 'light' read or flimsy text will almost certainly lead to a poorer essay and therefore a poorer mark.

Note ⋯⟩

Whilst this assignment is a pass/fail unit assessment, many teachers will grade the work, as with your writing task, in order that it becomes a potential piece of evidence should an appeal be required.

- Once you have chosen your text, read through it as soon as you can. This will help you form your initial response to the text.

- After you have formed your initial response, you should give considerable thought to how you will approach the essay. You will not be writing a general review.

- Before re-reading the book, decide which area you intend to focus on. This will necessitate consideration of issues such as theme, characterisation, structure and setting (see the examples below).

Choosing a Task

Consideration of theme: some students confuse theme and plot. The plot is the 'action', narrative, of a story; the theme is the topic that the text is concerned with. Themes you may come across might include issues such as growing-up, friendship and loyalty, family relationships, prejudice, violence, war and so on. A focus for a personal study essay would be to look at how the writer uses techniques such as characterisation, incident and setting to explore the theme of the novel.

A tighter focus for examining a text might be to look at how the writer develops a particular character throughout the story. Think about the character at the start of the novel and then consider what changes have taken place by the end. Your essay is about analysing the way in which the writer has brought about that change.

The writer's use of a particular of setting (for example a different time period) or structure/narrative stance may also create appropriate tasks for your essay. For example Anne Donovan's novel *Buddha Da* tells its story through different chapters being written from the viewpoint of three different characters, allowing us to gain different perspectives on the same sequence of events. Exploring the effect of this technique would provide a useful focus for a personal study task, in relation to this particular task.

- The more focused your task, the better your essay will be.

- Once you have decided on the focus of your essay, you should re-read the text and take notes of important points related to your main concern.

When you are finished, you are ready to tackle the writing stage.

As with the critical essay, the first stage is to create a title. This should reflect the purpose of your essay. For example:

In *Junk* the two main characters, Tar and Gemma, run away from a difficult home circumstance to create a new life for themselves. However, they are soon drawn into a world of drug addiction and petty crime. The book explores issues that many teenagers have to face in the modern world and it is a lively read. See page 111 for details.

In 1993, Toni Morrison became the first African-American woman to receive the Nobel Prize for Literature. She has been the winner of many literary awards and in 1998 *Beloved* won her the Pulitzer Prize. For more information about Toni Morrison, visit www.luminarium.org/ contemporary/tonimorrison/

See p. 87 for planning tips

←···· **Note**

How, in his novel *Junk*, Melvin Burgess uses the character of Tar to explore some of the problems facing young people today.
How the central character Tar learns from experience and develops into a well-adjusted adult in Melvin Burgess's novel *Junk*.

←···· **Note**

How the theme of racism is examined in the novel *Beloved* by Toni Morrison.
How Toni Morrison reveals the horror of slavery in her novel *Beloved*.

Having decided on a title, you can plan your essay in a similar fashion to the critical essay by ballooning the title and brainstorming ideas. Remember you are allowed to have an outline plan with you when you tackle the assignment.

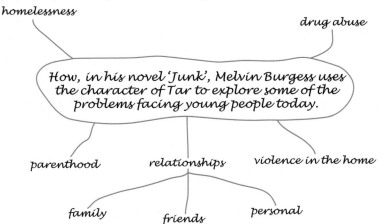

You can now write your outline plan, perhaps using topic sentences to create your structure. Your topic sentences should link to develop your line of thought in relation to the task created by your title.

You should then prepare additional notes to help you write your essay. These may be a list of key incidents in the story or perhaps thumbnail sketches of the key characters or important details relating to setting.

You should certainly have identified some key quotations to use in your essay and made a note of important themes explored by the text you have studied.

The work you do on this study can have a double benefit, as you will be allowed to use your chosen text as a potential choice for answering a critical essay assignment in the external examination. If you do this, of course, you have to respond to the task set in the exam paper and not rely on your original approach for the unit assessment.

Making Notes

As you re-read your text you should make notes as you go. Focus on issues such as incidents that reveal important insights into a situation or character; quotations that reveal personalities or key details; turning points in the plot; authorial comments linked to theme.

You should gather more notes than you need to write your essay as the process itself will develop your understanding of the text and then you will be able choose the most effective references for the essay itself.

Essentially you are gathering the evidence section of SEEC when you are making your notes.

Personal Study

Spoken Response

Getty Images / Photodisc blue

Introduction

You have the option to deliver your personal study assessment as a spoken piece. Uptake of this option in schools is likely to be relatively small given that it imposes some practical difficulties for teachers with large class sizes, not least being the time required to carry out the assessments. Some advice is given below, however, for those of you who wish to pursue this alternative.

Nature of the Assessment

The assessment takes the form of a delivered talk, which must last at least five minutes and be followed by in-depth questions from an audience of no less than three people. During the talk, all the performance criteria must be met. Those for Understanding, Analysis and Evaluation are essentially the same as for a written response (see page 100). Expression and Interaction with Audience are detailed below.

Expression

This relates to the performance side of the presentation. The speech should be clear and audible and effective use should be made of both verbal and non-verbal techniques to deliver the talk in a style appropriate to your purpose.

Interaction with Audience

This requires competent handling of questions asked and appropriate reactions to audience responses (e.g. pausing for laughter rather than simply ploughing on).

How to Tackle

As with any assessment, the key to individual presentation lies in adequate preparation. The topic of your talk, therefore, must be fully researched in order to allow you to deliver an effective presentation (see also Group Discussion advice on page 94).

Planning the talk is not dissimilar to planning an essay.

It is a good idea to create a planning title and then to create a mind map of your ideas and thoughts around this focus.

Like an essay, a talk will benefit enormously from having a clear structure.

List the various headings you intend to cover during the talk. Try not to make this list too long. It is more effective to have fewer points and to develop them thoroughly than it is to have a long list of topics that are skimmed over.

As a general guide, many of the best speeches are shaped around three key elements. Combined with your introduction and conclusion, this will create a sound structure for your planning.

Make sure that each element of the talk is introduced with a key statement, and that you link the sections together with appropriate phrases. As with the development of paragraphs in an essay, you should try to vary the way in which you support the different topics of your talk.

In the talk itself, be sure to support the content by appropriate and full use of body language (particularly gesture and facial expression), intonation and timing.

If you have said something amusing, for example, allow some time for audience reaction rather than charging straight on in a desperate hurry to be finished.

You must not, under any circumstances, simply bury your nose in your notes and read from a word-by-word script. It is legitimate to have notes in front of you but they should be abbreviated and act as an aid to memory rather than be the full content of the speech.

Before delivering your talk – practise. Use your parents, your brother/sister, the family dog, the mirror – whatever, as long as you rehearse the talk before delivering it. And practise does not mean only once! It can be very useful to tape yourself and then to listen to how the talk sounds.

Speak clearly and try to maintain an even pace. It is not a race!

Look at your audience and engage with them.

Show you are interested in what you are saying, as your enthusiasm will support the presentation.

And remember, with careful preparation, the talk will take care of itself.

Appendices

Appendix A

Alliteration – the use of the same consonant or vowel sound, usually at the beginning of words, e.g. 'soft snow settled on the silent scene', 'funny phone'.

Ambiguity – the idea that a word or phrase might mean more than one thing. Used in poetry to develop multiple levels of interpretation. For example 'And still *they* stand ...' (from line 13 of *The Horses* – see pages 72–73). 'Still' refers to the idea of 'not moving' and also the notion of 'yet', with the poet intending that the reader understands how both meanings apply in the context of the poem.

Clause – the grammatical term for a unit of language consisting of a verb and the words associated with it.

Cliché – an overused expression, often figurative, which has lost its impact because of its frequent use, e.g. 'A game of two halves'.

Conjunction – a word that links or joins together two words, phrases or clauses, e.g. 'and'.

Connotation – the ideas that might be suggested by a particular word choice, e.g. 'He strode into the room'. 'Strode' here suggests a sense of purpose.

Content – the ideas contained within a text.

Context – the words, phrases, sentences around the specified expression/word.

Course – a course comprises the individual units of a given subject, with their assessments, combined with the external examination.

Enjambment – where a poet runs a sentence or expression over more than one line without pause, e.g. consider the opening stanza of Norman MacCaig's *Visiting Hour* where this technique is used to support the movement being suggested:

> *The hospital smell*
> *combs my nostrils*
> *as they go bobbing along*
> *green and yellow corridors.*

Figurative Language – language that makes use of figures of speech and various techniques to add extra meaning to a text through a non-literal interpretation. Common figures of speech include metaphors, similes and personification.

Genre – a type or category of text, e.g. prose, drama, poetry, media.

Hyperbole – the proper term for deliberate exaggeration in writing, usually to provoke a reaction from the reader. '*If I have told you that once, I have told you a million times.*'

Image – the picture that is created by the words, often carrying some further meaning, e.g. the image of a rose has connotations of beauty.

Irony – this is a frequently used technique and it involves the idea of opposites but unlike sarcasm, explained later, it is not always negative in nature. Dramatic irony might involve a character saying something on stage that the audience knows will not come true. Irony can come from a situation where the intention of a character ends up with the opposite happening. It can be humorous, tragic, sad, fortunate or bitter:

> 'The irony of the situation was that the guide to understanding English only served to confuse the student more!'

Literal/Non-literal – literal is where a word means exactly what it says. Non-literal is where a word is being used metaphorically or is not meant to be taken completely at face value. For example, 'She has a very sharp mind' in a non-literal sense means she is very clever. Taken literally it would mean the person's brain had a physically sharp edge to it!

Litotes – deliberate understatement used to create a particular effect. For example, 'The school football squad is not the strongest group of players in the world', meaning it is one of the weakest!

Metaphor – **a comparison where the object being described is referred to directly as if it was something else, rather than being 'like' it. For example, 'The diamond-studded sky twinkled overhead' is comparing the stars to diamonds, but does not make a direct link in the way that a simile would: 'The stars, which were like diamonds in the sky, twinkled overhead.'**

Onomatopoeia – where a word makes the sound it is describing, e.g. 'sizzle', 'thud'.

Oxymoron – used to describe two words that are contradictory but, when used together express a clear meaning, e.g. 'bitter sweet'. ('Easy exam' might be a phrase that most students would regard as an oxymoron!)

Paradox – a puzzling contradiction of opposites; two contradictory ideas linked together. An example is the saying, 'You always hurt the one you love'.

Paragraph – a group of sentences about the same topic.

Parenthesis – a word or phrase that is not an essential part of the sentence, but is included to provide additional information or make an aside. Can be created by the use of two dashes, brackets or a pair of commas. Look back at the answer guide to *Parable of Wasted Talents* (see pages 32–36) for more information and examples.

Parts of Speech

    Adjective – adjectives describe nouns and are often found before the noun (or before another adjective if more than one is being used), e.g. the red, crumbling brick wall.

Note ····⫘

In a different context, red could be a noun – how a word is used defines its function.

    Adverb – a word which modifies a verb in some way, e.g. He ran quickly. 'Quickly' tells us more about the verb.

    Noun – a word which names things. There are different types of noun: proper nouns give the names of actual places or persons, e.g. Glasgow, Marianna, Britney Spears; common nouns refer to objects, e.g. desks, floor, rivers; collective nouns define groups of things, e.g. herd, class; abstract nouns define qualities, e.g. wisdom, kindness.

    Pronoun – a pronoun is a word which replaces a noun, e.g. he, she, it, they.

    Verb – a verb is often referred to as a 'doing word'; the word which denotes the action, e.g. run, cry, shout.

Personification – where an inanimate object is described as having qualities normally associated with something that is alive: 'The wind whistled down the alley' or 'Winter spread its icy grip over the fields and hills'.

Portmanteau – a term first used by Lewis Carroll to describe a word that has been created by joining together two existing words, e.g. eugenics and genesis to create eugenesis; or lithe and slimy to give slithy.

Punctuation

Apostrophe (') – used to indicate where a letter has been missed out when two words are contracted together, e.g. it's = it is; or to show when something belongs to another (shows possession), e.g. Sheila's house = the house that belongs to Sheila.

Colon (:) – used to introduce a list or where the second part of the sentence elaborates or explains in some way the first part.

Comma (,) – used to create a pause in a sentence and to break up a list of items. Also used in parenthesis, as explained in the answer section to *Parable of Wasted Talents* (see pages 32–36).

Exclamation mark (!) – used to indicate when a word, phrase, clause or sentence should be read as indicating surprise or special emphasis.

Full stop (.) – used to mark the end of a sentence.

Inverted commas (' ') – used to indicate direct speech and to indicate titles. Also used to show where a word is not to be taken literally as its usage is slightly unusual in the given context. Single (' ') or double (" ") inverted commas are usually equally acceptable.

Question mark (?) – used to mark the end of a sentence that asks a question.

Semi-colon (;) – used to link what might otherwise be two separate sentences but where a close link is desired. Can also be used to break up a list, especially where it is a list of phrases/clauses rather than single words.

Register – the term used to describe groups of words or phrases that are associated with a particular genre, e.g. 'Dearly Beloved ... brethren ... amen' would be an example of a religious register.

Rhyme – words that have the same sound, used most often at the end of lines in poetry:

As virtuous men pass mildly away,	a
And whisper to their souls, to go,	b
Whilst some of their sad friends do say,	a
The breath goes now, and some say, no...	b

A Valediction Forbidding Mourning
John Donne

Rhythm – the beat within a line of poetry, created through stressed syllables. Consider this limerick:

There **was** a young **man** from the **West**
Who **thought** he was **sim**ply the **best**
But there **came** from the **East**
A **strange** kind of **beast**
And **his**tory **tells** us the **rest**!

The underlined syllables are stressed, giving us the traditional rhythm of a limerick:

Da **da** da da **da** da da **da**
Da **da** da da **da** da da **da**
Da da **da**, da da **da**
Da **da**, da da **da**
Da **da** da da **da** da da **da**.

Sarcasm – to do with the tone of a text or expression. It is usually identified when the opposite of what is being said is what is actually meant. Sarcasm is often a criticism of some sort, for example saying 'That was very clever!' when you actually mean 'That was incredibly stupid!'

Sentence – a group of words that make sense; almost always centred on a verb.

Simile – where two or more things are compared directly using the word 'like' or 'as' to link the comparison, e.g. 'The stars were like diamonds in the sky.'

Stanza – refers to poetry where groups of lines are used to structure the poem.

Syllable – a group of letters that combine to make a sound (think of the party game 'Charades'). For example, beautiful has three syllables – beau - ti - ful – but ugly has only two – ug - ly.

Symbol – an idea or object that represents more than just its literal self, e.g. light is often a symbol of hope.

Syntax – the order of words in a sentence. Close reading questions often ask about sentences where the normal word order (of subject, verb, and then additional information) has not been followed. A writer may decide to change this structure in order to create a particular effect or emphasis: for example, by beginning with an adverb, 'Nervously, the candidate entered the exam room'.

Theme – the central concern of a text; the idea being explored rather than the events of the text.

Tone – the feel, sense of atmosphere suggested by words; in speech the sound of someone's voice conveys tone quite clearly but its meaning is essentially the same whether the words are spoken or written. Look back at the close reading passages for examples of tone (see pages 8–43).

Unit – National Qualification courses in English are divided into three separate units: Language, Literature and Personal Study. A student can be accredited with passes in a single unit but to achieve a course pass all three units must be passed as well as the external examination.

Verse – refers to separate sections of a poem, often with a distinct rhyming scheme.

Appendix B

(Paul Trummer)/Getty Images

Novels tend to be the most popular choice amongst students for independent study, although you can also choose between non-fiction, poetry and drama. The list below contains a number of suggestions that are popular with teenage readers. If you wish to find out more about particular titles you can either visit a bookshop or use the internet. Most bookshop websites include readers' reviews and a brief synopsis of the book in question.

It is important to select a text that you will enjoy reading because personal engagement is one of the key issues in assessing the quality of critical essay responses, so take your time and choose wisely.

Clearly this list is not exhaustive and it is really only offered by way of a sample of the kind of books you should be looking at. Your teacher will be able to offer you sound advice in your final choice.

Chinua Achebe, *Things Fall Apart* (Penguin Books; ISBN: 0141186887)
> This novel has become a modern classic. It tells the powerful story of Okonkwo, a proud member of the Ibo tribe, and how the culture of his people becomes threatened by the emergence of white colonialism in his country. Lots of material to write about.

Rachel Anderson, *The War Orphan* (Oxford University Press; ISBN: 019275095x)
> Simon's family adopt a Vietnamese war orphan, Ha, who has suffered terribly. But Simon has to discover much about himself as he struggles to cope with his new brother's nightmares.

Jane Austen, *Emma* (Penguin Books; ISBN: 0140434151)
> A classic comedy of manners in which the central character is forced to face up to the reality of relationships.

Iain Banks, *The Wasp Factory* (Abacus; ISBN: 0349101779)
> Iain Banks is now a major writer and this 1984 work, his first novel, remains a best seller today. Described as a 'gothic horror story' it tells the violent tale of Frank who lives in a remote part of Scotland with his father and both have their dark secrets from each other.

Pat Barker, *The Ghost Road* (Penguin Books; ISBN: 0140236287)
> Winner of the 1995 Booker Prize, this book, part of a series, mixes fact and fiction as it looks at the life of Sarah, a munitions worker, and that of Wilfred Owen, the First World War poet (author of *Dulce Et Decorum Est*).

Greg Bear, *Eon* (Gollancz; ISBN: 0575073160)
> A complex science-fiction epic that examines one possibility for our future. One for fans of the genre.

Emily Brontë, *Wuthering Heights* (Penguin Books; ISBN: 0140434186)
> The classic love story of Catherine and Heathcliffe. Like most classics this novel requires a certain staying power but it certainly provides a rich resource for critical essay writing.

Christopher Brookmyre, *Quite Ugly One Morning* (Abacus; ISBN: 0349108854)
> A thriller written with the usual panache from this Scottish writer who lays bare the darker side of human behaviour but always manages to raise a smile from the reader whilst doing so.

Melvin Burgess, *Junk* (Puffin Books; ISBN: 0140380191)
> The gritty story of Tar and Gemma, two teenage runaways who become involved in serious drug-taking. Popular with teenagers because of the way it tackles real issues in an uncompromising way.

Truman Capote, *Breakfast at Tiffany's* (Penguin Books; ISBN: 0141182792)
> This tale of Holly Golightly, a seemingly carefree and stunningly beautiful young woman, offers wide scope for character analysis in a critical response. A fairly short book.

Amit Chaudhuri, *Freedom Song* (Picador; ISBN: 0330344242)
> A young boy's stay with relatives in Calcutta precipitates an exploration of family relationships as serious efforts are made to 'marry off' a difficult relative.

Anita Desai, *Fasting, Feasting* (Vintage; ISBN: 0099289636)
> An examination of the contrast between two cultures, India and North America, through the lives of a brother and sister, Arun and Uma, and their strict parents.

Kiran Desai, *Hullabaloo in the Guava Orchard* (Faber and Faber; ISBN: 0571195717)
> Sampath has been a bit of a failure in life until one day when he climbs into a monkey tree and finds unexpected fame as a saintly guru! Gently humorous look at aspects of life in India.

Charles Dickens, *A Tale of Two Cities* (Penguin Books; ISBN: 0140437304)
> There are a lot of words in a Dickens' novel but he was a master storyteller and those who tackle this book will discover the truth of this.

Roddy Doyle, *The Commitments* (Vintage; ISBN: 0749391685)
> Part of the Barrytown trilogy that looks at the lives of the Rabbite family from North Dublin. This first tale is that of Jimmy and his attempt to form a rock band. It examines issues such as the individual versus the group and like the other books, *The Snapper* and *The Van*, it is quite an easy book to read whilst still offering the student a number of sound points to write about.

Roddy Doyle, *The Woman Who Walked Into Doors* (Vintage; ISBN: 0749395990)
> A more sombre book from Roddy Doyle which charts the chaotic life of a woman driven to alcoholism by the abuse she suffers from her husband.

Sebastian Faulks, *Birdsong* (Vintage; ISBN: 0099387913)
> A challenging book in terms of its scope but brilliantly written and well worth tackling by students. It contains more than one storyline although the central narrative concerns Stephen Wraysford and the impact that the First World War has upon him.

John Fowles, *The Collector* (Vintage; ISBN: 009974371x)
> A chilling study of the kidnap of a young woman and the subsequent relationship/duel between the victim and the perpetrator.

Brian Friel, *Dancing at Lughnasa* (Faber and Faber; ISBN: 0571144799)
> A priest returns from the missions to his family bosom in Ireland, but it appears that he learned more from Africa than he imparted. A comedy with some very sharp edges to it. (Drama)

Jostein Gaarder, *Sophie's World* (Phoenix; ISBN: 1857992911)
'Who are you? Where does the world come from?' If you want to know the answer to these deep philosophical questions this book is for you – but be warned, it is not an easy journey.

Janice Galloway, *The Trick is to Keep Breathing* (Minerva; ISBN: 0749391731)
Award-winning novel from one of Scotland's best-known writers. The story revolves around a West of Scotland drama teacher with more than her fair share of psychological problems.

Jamila Gavin, *Coram Boy* (Mammoth; ISBN: 0749732687)
Historical drama set in 18th century England, focusing on the fate and fortune of two parentless boys with very different family histories. A rewarding read for students.

Maggie Graham, *Sitting Among the Eskimos* (Review; ISBN: 0747268304)
A modern tale of a working-class housewife who struggles to complete a degree at University whilst still being a full-time mother and wife.

Kazuo Ishiguro, *The Remains of the Day* (Faber and Faber; ISBN: 0571154913)
1989 Booker Prize-winning tale of an elderly butler on a whimsical car journey. Quite difficult.

Robin Jenkins, *The Changeling* (Canongate Classics; ISBN: 0862412285)
Tom Curdie is what people would describe as a ned. But one of his teachers thinks that there may be more to him, or is the teacher just on an ego trip? Tom goes on holiday with the teacher's family, leaving behind his Glasgow home, but what lies in front? A relatively straightforward book to tackle.

Catherine Johnson, *Other Colours* (Livewire; ISBN: 0704349450)
This is from the Livewire for Teenage Readers series and, like most of the books in the collection, it appeals greatly to young adults. In this novel Louise runs away from her mother and stepfather to find her own identity and ambitions on the streets of London.

Brian Keaney, *Bitter Fruit* (Orchard Books; ISBN: 1841210056)
Rebecca's father dies in a car accident and the teenager is forced to come to terms with many of life's realities more quickly than she would have otherwise.

Lois Keith, *A Different Life* (Livewire; ISBN: 0704349469)
Another from the Livewire series which tells the story of Libby Starling who becomes disabled at the age of fifteen. Suddenly she has to reassess her life and her attitude. More crucially she has to deal with the attitudes of others.

James Kelman, *A Chancer* (Picador; ISBN: 0330296647)
An early work from an author who constantly challenges the establishment to recognise the reality of working-class life, particularly in the West of Scotland. Here the main character likes a wee bet, now and again. Quite difficult.

Ken Kesey, *One Flew Over the Cuckoo's Nest* (Picador; ISBN: 0330491903)
A complex but gripping modern classic. The psychiatric hospital where McMurphy finds himself is a microcosm of American society and through the regime depicted, the characterisation, and McMurphy's struggle for his individualism, Kesey offers the reader an abundance of food for thought.

Federico Garcia Lorca, *The House of Bernarda Alba* (Nick Hern Books; ISBN: 1854594591)
> A classic tale of a repressive household and the impact that an overbearing mother has on her daughters. (Drama)

Bernard MacLaverty, *Cal* (Penguin Books; ISBN: 0140817891)
> Set in the troubles of Northern Ireland this is a love story riddled with Cal's guilt. An accessible text for all students.

Bernard MacLaverty, *Grace Notes* (Vintage; ISBN: 0099778017)
> Catherine has to struggle with the break up of her relationship, her estranged father's death and her post-natal depression. She finds solace in her ability as a composer. The novel's structure offers a good starting point for critical appraisal.

Frank McCourt, *Angela's Ashes* (Flamingo; ISBN: 0006510345)
> An autobiographical account of the writer's early life in Limerick and the appalling poverty his family faced. The only warning to be considered about books such as this is that they are not novels and therefore a slightly different approach is required when writing about them.

Ian McEwan, *The Child in Time* (Vintage; ISBN: 0099755017)
> Examines the impact on a young couple of their child being snatched away from them.

William McIlvanney, *Laidlaw* (Sceptre; ISBN: 0340576901)
> The first of McIlvanney's Laidlaw books in which the detective tracks down the murderer of a young girl, exploring various aspects of Glasgow life in the process. A good detective story as well as plenty of material to write about in an essay.

Toni Morrison, *Beloved* (Vintage; ISBN: 0099273934)
> Possibly Toni Morrison's finest book. A searing indictment of the horrors of slavery told in a way that will grip the reader. This is not an easy read but it is highly rewarding for the students who can master its complexities.

Toni Morrison, *The Bluest Eye* (Vintage; ISBN: 0099759918)
> A more straightforward tale from Morrison about a young girl, Pecola, who longs for blue eyes like her white friends. A novel about identity.

Millie Murray, *Sorrelle* (Livewire; ISBN: 070434954x)
> Again from the Livewire series, about a young black woman and her Asian boyfriend and the problems they face from both families.

Janet Paisley, *Not for Glory* (Canongate; ISBN: 1841951749)
> A series of interlinked stories set in a small village in central Scotland. Paisley examines the lives of a host of related characters through the unusual structure of this book.

Tony Parsons, *Man and Boy* (HarperCollins; ISBN: 0006512135)
> The story of a father who has to learn how to care for his son after his own infidelity leads to the departure of his wife. A clever and accessible book about relationships and responsibilities.

Ian Rankin, *Tooth and Nail* (Orion; ISBN: 0752809407)
> Part of the Rebus series which is very popular at the moment. In this tale Rebus heads south to track down the 'Wolfman'.

Ken Saro-Wiwa, *Lemona's Tale* (Penguin Books; ISBN: 0140260862)
> The tragic tale of Lemona's life and her exploitation by various men; Saro-Wiwa's tale is a searing indictment of chauvinist attitudes and state corruption.

Sir Walter Scott, *Rob Roy* (Penguin Books; ISBN: 0140435549)
> Published in 1817, this famous historical romance tells the tale of Rob Roy MacGregor, leader of the MacGregor clan and forced into becoming an outlaw because of his suspected support for the Jacobite rebellion of 1715.

George Bernard Shaw, *Pygmalion* (Penguin Books; ISBN: 0140437894)
> Written to be read as well as acted, Pygmalion is the tale of Eliza Dolittle, a social experiment for two eminent gentlemen who wager about the possibility of turning this flower-girl into a lady. (Drama)

Joe Simpson, *Touching the Void* (Vintage; ISBN: 0099771012)
> A story of the difficulties the author and his climbing partner faced on their descent from the top of the 21,000 foot Siula Grande mountain. Told from two perspectives, this is a gripping account of the challenges confronted in the face of death.

Alan Spence, *The Magic Flute* (Phoenix; ISBN: 1857997816)
> Tam learns to play the flute to join an Orange band but his musical talent changes the shape of his life. Set in the 1960s and 1970s, Spence's narrative reflects the Scotland of that period and offers students a wealth of material to focus on.

Ena Lamont-Stewart, *Men Should Weep* (Samuel French; ISBN: 0573018383)
> A classic play set in the Glasgow of the past but still relevant to the Glasgow of today as it examines the role of women in the family and society generally. (Drama)

Meera Syal, *Anita and Me* (Flamingo; ISBN: 0006548768)
> A memoir of growing up in the sixties when the author was part of the only Punjabi family in a small mining village. Humorous and skillfully told.

Donna Tartt, *The Secret History* (Penguin Books; ISBN: 0140167773)
> A murder story where a group of elite students share a secret guilt. It is extremely well written and has very effective characterisation.